The Dyslexia-Friendly Teacher's Toolkit

The Dyslexia-Friendly Teacher's Toolkit

Strategies for Teaching Students 3–18

Barbara Pavey, Margaret Meehan & Sarah Davis

SAGE | AdvantEDGE Teacher Resources

Los Angeles | London | New Delhi
Singapore | Washington DC | Melbourne

Originally published in 2013 by

SAGE

Los Angeles | London | New Delhi
Singapore | Washington DC | Melbourne

SAGE Publications Ltd
1 Oliver's Yard
55 City Road
London EC1Y 1SP

This SAGE AdvantEDGE edition published in 2017 by

SAGE | AdvantEDGE Teacher Resources

SAGE Publications India Pvt Ltd
B-1/I-1, Mohan Cooperative Industrial Area
Mathura Road
New Delhi 110 044

Published by Vivek Mehra for SAGE Publications India Pvt Ltd and printed at Avantika Printers Pvt Ltd, New Delhi.

ISBN: 978-93-860-6254-3 (PB)

This book is dedicated to
Dorothy Gilroy
a tireless advocate for dyslexic students

Contents

List of figures and tables

Figures

* = Photocopiable resource

Tables

List of abbreviations

BDA	British Dyslexia Association
BECTA	British Educational and Communications Technology
DAMP	disorder of attention, movement and perception
DCD	developmental coordination disorder
DCFS	Department for Children, Schools and Families
DfES	Department for Education and Skills
EAL	English as an Additional Language
ICT	information and communication technology
IRI	Informal Reading Inventory
MIS	Meares-Irlen syndrome
NACCCE	National Advisory Committee on Creative and Cultural Education
NALDIC	National Association for Language Development in the Curriculum
NCBIDA	North California Branch, International Dyslexia Association
Ofsted	Office for Standards in Education
PhAB	Phonological Assessment Battery
RTI	Response To Intervention
SASC	SpLD Assessment Standards Committee
SEN	special educational needs
SENCO	special educational needs coordinator
SpLD	specific learning difficulty
TA	teaching assistant
VAK	visual, auditory, kinaesthetic

About the authors

Barbara Pavey is a lecturer in higher education, training dyslexia specialists in the North of England. She has been an inclusion and special education practitioner for a wide range of student ages and learning settings. She has been a SENCO and a local authority administrative manager in SEN, and holds a rights-based view of education, focusing on helping practitioners to enable pupils and students to make progress.

Margaret Meehan has worked in the field of dyslexia and specific learning difficulties for over 15 years. Initially supporting dyslexic students who experienced difficulties with mathematics and science, she delivers specialist tuition to students across all disciplines and at present is the Coordinator of Specialist Tuition at Swansea University. Her training in advanced counselling skills enables Margaret to understand how specific learning difficulties impinge on every aspect of daily living.

Sarah Davis is an early years leading teacher working in North Yorkshire, with over 25 years' teaching experience; she is also a dyslexia specialist. She is currently part of an extended Every Child a Talker project, and focuses upon early language and literacy.

Acknowledgements

The authors would like to thank contributors whose words, experience and insight inform this book, including Gillian Trivasse, Geraldine Hills, Mike Juggins and our anonymised originators of words and stories. We thank Nicola Owens and Kerry Rough at Pearson, and Mo Brown at GL, for information about dyslexia assessment materials. We also thank David Wilcox at WY Education Equipment Ltd for information about Attribute Blocks.

We are grateful to Ted Glynn, Janice Wearmouth and Mere Berryman for their permission to include Pause, Prompt, Praise, and for the kind advice they gave us. We are also grateful to the Dyspraxia Foundation for allowing us to include their guidelines for homework.

We would like to acknowledge that the Audit tool (Appendix 1) follows similar items to those developed in Pavey (2007), and Pavey, Meehan and Waugh (2010). Finally, we would like to thank the editorial team at Sage, particularly Jude Bowen and Miriam Davey, for their patience and wise advice.

Introduction

Within the dyslexia field of study there are competing philosophical approaches and causal theories. The proliferation of dyslexia Internet sites also testifies to the international importance given to the issues concerning difficulty in literacy acquisition. The main purpose of this book is to explore the present position and take forward the ideas and practices generated by the Dyslexia-friendly initiative, applying them to practice that helps teachers and learners.

The Dyslexia-friendly view proposes that practices designed to help dyslexic learners can help all learners. The urge to do better for students, driven also by national projects to improve literacy levels, has meant that there is now much valuable Dyslexia-friendly practice in classrooms. Neil MacKay's original 'dyslexia friendly' concept, subsequently adopted by the British Dyslexia Association (1999) can now be found in many mainstream schools.

Nevertheless, there will always be some students who experience a greater degree of difficulty, and so teachers and learning support assistants continue to seek solutions for the educational difficulties characterising dyslexia. A Dyslexia-friendly practitioner is a responsive person, using their input to gain new information about learners' approaches, preferences and skills, and turning this new information into teaching that will aid their learners. A Dyslexia-friendly practitioner understands that their approaches benefit the wide range of learners, including high achievers and also learners who struggle to make progress more generally.

The chapters are focused upon 'tools', with additional discussion about present dyslexia understanding, expressed in terms of Dyslexia-friendly practice. Each chapter starts with good practice points and includes case studies, something to try and examples of learners' own words, plus ICT, homework and revision ideas. Strategic and practical activities are suggested for different phases of education. Chapters conclude with a five-step process aimed at helping educators move towards a Dyslexia-friendly pedagogy, plus useful websites and recommended reading.

It is important to acknowledge that dyslexia is owned by the people who experience it and by those who are close to them. Accordingly the co-authors trust that this book will be useful to practitioners, but also to parents and carers, students, and learners of all ages who experience dyslexia in their own right.

1

Understanding learners with dyslexia

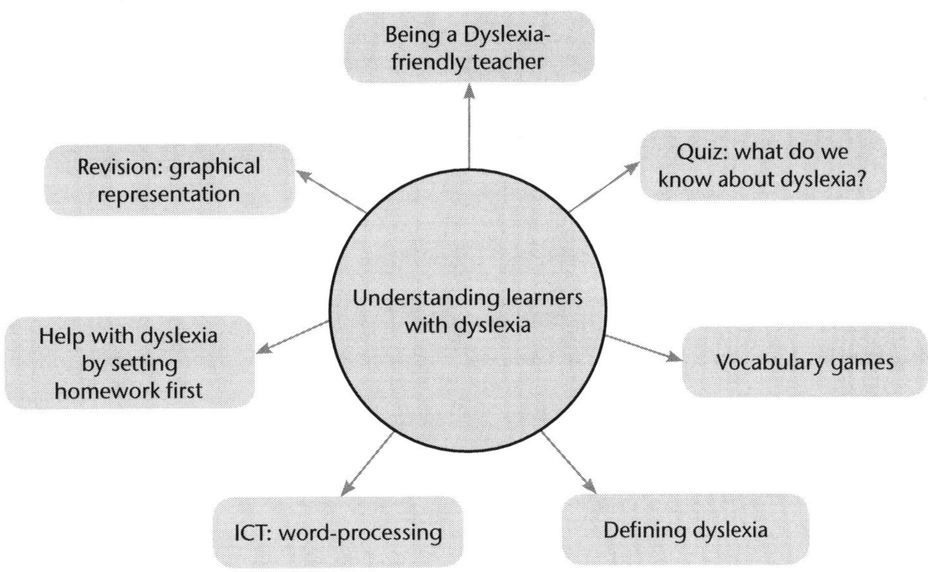

The main ways of talking about dyslexia fall within a medical-psychological (deficit-based) view and a socially constructed view. In education, dyslexia discussion is often about how to improve the learning power and skills of dyslexic students; this can become a discourse of deficit. In seeking to help learners, a Dyslexia-friendly view does not consider dyslexia characteristics as deficits to be discussed in terms of student failings. Instead it promotes commitment to improving our learning environments. We seek to develop awareness of approaches that will help students to manage their learning and to achieve appropriately.

Good Practice Points: Being a Dyslexia-friendly teacher

A great deal more is known about dyslexia than used to be the case, and a great deal of good practice may be found in schools incorporated into practitioners' daily routines.

A Dyslexia-friendly teacher's professional knowledge is a combination of attitude, understanding, technique and empathy. If we do not experience dyslexia ourselves, it may help to adopt a 'dyslexia proxy' by reflecting on our experience of some other, personal difficulty in our schooling. To be Dyslexia-friendly we can:

1. Make ourselves familiar with the characteristics of dyslexia.
2. Appreciate the importance of the learning environment.
3. See dyslexia as a whole-school concern.
4. Keep updating our own knowledge.
5. Use Dyslexia-friendly approaches, including multisensory practices.
6. Notice individual students' preferred ways of learning, providing opportunities for success.
7. Connect new learning to previous, secure learning, and then rehearse and revisit.
8. Allow a variety of methods for recording work.
9. Understand that there are good days and bad days, appreciating that this is not deliberate avoidance or laziness in a learner.
10. Protect students' feelings, realising that literacy activity may be fearful for some learners.
11. Recognise that sometimes it is two steps forward and one step back – or vice versa!
12. Provide dyslexic students with opportunities for success.

Dyslexia is a heterogeneous concept, so we can say that no two dyslexic learners are the same. In addition, whatever the individual characteristics of dyslexia, environmental elements of all types provide meaningful influences that cannot be fully assessed, since they are the effect of lives as they are lived. Nevertheless, there is now a degree of confidence in common characteristics among most dyslexic learners. Foremost among these is the recognition of phonological difficulty and/or reduced speed of processing, and memory difficulties, all characterised by a lack of automaticity. Additional characteristics, such as sequencing or organisational difficulties, may or may not fall within formal definitions of dyslexia.

Quiz: What do we know about dyslexia?

Dyslexia knowledge is increasing all the time and is more widely dispersed. The quiz presented in Figure 1.1 is a photocopiable resource for self-reflection or training. We suggest giving out the blank version for people to work on individually or together, and then giving out the same sheet with the answers inked in. This provides information quickly and avoids using time on covering material that people already know; it may also update earlier knowledge. It is noticeable that some of the answers are 'unsure' until further research has clarified the issues. The quiz also highlights the amount of misunderstanding that may be found about dyslexia. The answers, in terms of current knowledge, are:

1 False	10 Sometimes	18 True
2 False	11 True	19 False
3 False	12 Unsure	20 Sometimes
4 True	13 Unsure	21 False
5 False	14 False	22 False
6 Sometimes	15 False	23 True
7 False	16 Sometimes	24 True
8 Sometimes	17 False	25 Sometimes
9 Sometimes		

	True	**False**	**Some-times**	**Unsure**
1. There is an agreed theoretical understanding of dyslexia				
2. There is an agreed definition of dyslexia				
3. Dyslexia affects mostly boys				
4. Dyslexia can be inherited				
5. There is a (single) dyslexia gene				
6. People with dyslexia work better with tinted paper				
7. Dyslexia can be cured				
8. The main difficulty is reading (decoding)				
9. The main difficulty is spelling				
10. The main difficulty is written expression				
11. The main difficulty is that literacy skills do not become automatic				
12. The main difficulty is memory				
13. The main difficulty is speed of processing				
14. The main difficulty is letter reversals				
15. Dyslexia is completely different from 'ordinary' reading delay				
16. Learners with dyslexia have strengths in other areas				
17. Dyslexia is a myth				
18. Dyslexic learners experience more fatigue				
19. Dyslexic learners are best placed in low achieving sets/ groups				
20. Dyslexic learners need to sit at the front				
21. Extra time in exams is for checking spelling				
22. It is unfair to other learners to ask a dyslexic child for less output				
23. The experience of dyslexia relates to the language used				
24. Dyslexic learners are disadvantaged by surprise literacy tasks, e.g. reading aloud, writing on a board, a quiz				
25. People with dyslexia are very intelligent in other ways				

Figure 1.1 What do we know about dyslexia? A quiz

Dyslexia is now largely, but not exclusively, understood to be a difficulty with significance for the language centre of a brain. Reduced activation is now seen as a key factor rather than physiological abnormality or deficit in a brain's structure. Dyslexic students may also experience problems with mathematics, musical notation and motor control. This last, where it impacts upon handwriting difficulties, may be discussed in the UK as part of an individual's expression of dyslexia or be associated with dyspraxia; it may also be separately identified as dysgraphia.

In written work dyslexic students may rely on a safe vocabulary, which will mean that they may not use words that will demonstrate the sophistication of their understanding. This does not mean that they may not enjoy exploring and using an extended vocabulary, and with encouragement students can go on to use this in writing. There are vocabulary games available which are literacy exercises presented in an appealing way, but the three games below are offered as helpful to dyslexic students because they do not put an individual in the spotlight. They do not rely on writing and spelling, and most importantly they are intended to be fun. In this way they help dyslexic students to get the matter of vocabulary under control.

Something to Try: Vocabulary games

- **Today's Target Word.** A teacher sets a target word and students using that word in the course of the lesson receive praise or applause or a reward of some kind. The teacher identifies the word at the start of the lesson and provides the opportunity for students to ask for an explanation, and to understand that they are not being asked to give an example of how the word might be used, or demonstrate their knowledge of the word, or talk about similar words or rhyming words (although actually these would be useful vocabulary-extending activities). Instead they are being asked to slide the word into conversation or discussion; this is a far more creative task, and one that requires students to listen carefully. Use of the word generates praise and applause.
- **Vocabulary War.** The class is divided in two. Students in one group choose a word and challenge the other group to define and/or put it in context. Students can confer to find challenging examples to nominate, or to check with each other what would be the correct answer, allowing for further focused chat about the word. Students might well nominate, for the other side, the most difficult and convoluted word they could think of, which would make it more fun. The teacher is the arbiter and points can be given to either side for correct usage.
- **Headlines.** The teacher nominates three seemingly random words and students have to make a headline out of them, preferably comic or credibility-stretching headlines, but ones that make sense. Again, this can be done in groups or in 'sides', challenging each other.

Defining dyslexia

In the UK professional support endorses the definition published in the Rose Report of 2009, *Identifying and Teaching Children and Young People with Dyslexia and Literacy Difficulties* – a publicly available resource. While this is described as a 'working definition', it is embraced by the major dyslexia organisations. Rose's definition begins:

> Dyslexia is a learning difficulty that primarily affects the skills involved in accurate and fluent word reading and spelling. (Rose 2009: 30)

Referring also to the relative strengths that some people with dyslexia may experience, the British Dyslexia Association (BDA) augments this definition:

> In addition to these characteristics, the BDA acknowledges the visual and auditory processing difficulties that some individuals with dyslexia can experience, and points out that dyslexic readers can show a combination of abilities and difficulties that affect the learning process. (BDA, n.d.)

Reading comprehension and written expression are not included in Rose's definition, although they are explored later in the report where each subsequent element of the definition is discussed in more detail. The definition focuses upon six elements, shown here in italics:

> *Characteristic features of dyslexia are difficulties in phonological awareness, verbal memory and verbal processing speed.*

While these elements are 'reliable markers of dyslexia' (Rose, 2009: 33), this is not the same as saying that all these characteristics must be present in order for dyslexia to be identified. Some dyslexic learners do not have a clearly discerned phonological difficulty when tested. The word 'characteristic' does not mean compulsorily present; the definition allows for the possibility of variation among dyslexic learners.

> *Dyslexia occurs across the range of intellectual abilities.*

A welcome addition to earlier definitions, this reduces the possibility of under-identification and lack of Dyslexia-friendly intervention for some learners. It accords with the principle that good teaching for dyslexia is good teaching for everyone.

> *It is best thought of as a continuum, not a distinct category, and there are no clear cut-off points.*

This represents an important development in dyslexia understanding. While there has been no difficulty with the understanding that dyslexia itself falls within a range, typically characterised as mild, moderate or severe dyslexia, this point goes further. The report continues:

> *Until recently a child was deemed ether to have or not have dyslexia. It is now recognised that there is no sharp dividing line between having a learning difficulty and not having it. (p. 34)*

Debate has focused upon whether dyslexia forms a discrete category of reading difficulty/disability, or whether the term describes the extreme expression of traits that are continuously distributed among people. The above explanation identifies dyslexia as representing the most challenging end of the range of general reading acquisition, where it becomes disabling. However there is no agreement as to where this tipping point occurs.

> *Co-occurring difficulties may be seen in aspects of language, motor coordination, mental calculation, concentration and personal organisation, but these are not, by themselves, markers of dyslexia.*

There is increasing interest in the other characteristics that many dyslexic students may experience; some specialists think that most dyslexic students experience complicating difficulties.

> *A good indication of the severity and persistence of dyslexic difficulties can be gained by examining how the individual responds or has responded to well-founded intervention.*

Earlier definitions understood that dyslexia was characterised by its intractability and the term 'developmental dyslexia' has long been used to distinguish it from acquired dyslexia. Dyslexic learners today may be identified in research as demonstrating the literacy characteristics of younger, less experienced readers. While we now understand dyslexia as describing the extreme end of a regular distribution of reading acquisition, there is a difference between a reader who is delayed because they are untutored and one who experiences dyslexia and that difference concerns intractability. With regular skilled teaching a delayed, untutored reader will catch up, but dyslexic learners will continue to have difficulty in some areas of literacy, even if it is not immediately apparent in their reading.

Case Study: Larry

Sometimes dyslexic difficulties are less obvious, reflecting dyslexia's location within a range.

Larry learned to read early on, by an unusual route. His grandparents owned a bookshop and made sure that Larry had access to many beautiful books. He would look at the print while stories were read to him, the words were pointed out and the stories were discussed. At school, because he could read, there was no cause for concern about his literacy. However, Larry's spelling was not as good as his reading, and his written work was slow; he rarely produced more than one or two sentences.

Larry's reports were consistently written as variations on the theme 'could do better'. As far as Larry was concerned, he was trying his hardest and did not know how he could do better. He read slowly and had to read every word; he knew he was trying hard, but could not explain to his parents why his results were disappointing.

In spite of a strong start, Larry's reading skill did not develop to a sophisticated level. However, he was good at guessing the context of what he read, preferring practical, illustrated texts to fiction and novels. As far as his teachers were concerned, he remained a person who simply did not engage well with literacy-based work. He left school as soon as he was old enough. As an adult, Larry developed his own successful gardening business and now pays others to do clerical and administrative work for him.

Commentary: How might a Dyslexia-friendly teacher and school support Larry?

Larry's situation reflects how a learner may experience dyslexia which remains unidentified. Is Larry dyslexic? In Larry's case, his learning history suggests that he missed out on learning phonological strategies that would help him to decode unfamiliar words, but the seriousness of his difficulty, and its persistence, suggests that this is due to more than lack of tutoring.

Increasingly, knowledge of dyslexia makes it easier to identify a student with severe dyslexia who, in spite of best efforts, remains at an immature level of literacy. It is often the case that students develop their own strategies to help them manage literacy tasks. These may remain hidden, and there may be insights, surprises and interesting ideas in store for a teacher who asks a student how they actually go about a literacy task. If at a later date they are engaged with higher level study, students with this profile may reach a point where self-developed strategies are not enough. It may not be until this point that they are identified as dyslexic, and then support can be provided and entitlements met.

Student Voices: Neil

A Dyslexia-friendly teacher sees a student's response to teaching as a guide; it tells a teacher about the things students find difficult and the best ways of helping. Here is the voice of Neil, an adult, who could have been like Larry at school:

> *I still, now, go to write a word and I'll start off at the back, and I'll work my way to the back. It's the same with my reading. Sometimes I'll write half the word, and write the other half of the word, and put a little bit in. When I'm reading especially, sometimes it's just one line, constantly, I just can't break the words up. I make it up instead – I get on with it.* (Neil, an adult)

What might a Dyslexia-friendly teacher learn from this?

1. There is a need to investigate what Neil means when he says *I'll start off at the back, and I'll work my way to the back.* Is this a verbal slip-up, a mistake, or his actual strategy? A teacher might expect a linear progression along a certain literacy learning route, so would only know about these things from asking Neil or from observing him closely and sensitively.
2. The way Neil approaches the task of writing a word has nothing to do with the way in which a teacher might expect it to be approached. Some might say this was incorrect, yet Neil can work it out his own way. He puts in the bits he knows, then has a look at it and if he is not satisfied he adjusts it.
3. In reading Neil tells us that he has difficulty breaking words into their component parts – 'segmenting' as it is described in literacy teaching. This shows a need for an intervention that will teach this skill in a focused way.
4. If Neil does not know the word, he will substitute something and carry on – this is a good coping strategy for him.
5. His own analysis shows that Neil is well aware of his difficulties and the ways he copes with them.

It is quite possible that Neil would have spent his school years in the lower subject sets. This is a common pattern and an unhelpful one; dyslexic learners should not be in lower sets because of their literacy. They should be supported at a level commensurate with their overall ability, but this can be hard for schools to arrange. Dyslexia-friendly processes are helpful throughout the school; nevertheless, there are always some students who will need additional help.

Information and Communication Technology: Word-processing

There are many advantages for dyslexia learners in the use of ICT, but the most common usage is for producing written work. In 2000 Sally McKeown summed up the value to dyslexic learners of using ICT, particularly word-processing:

- Written tasks are more easily managed.
- The alphabet is displayed on keys, aiding memory and removing reliance on correct letter formation.
- Written work is therefore more legible.
- Presentation is better so that unfavourable judgements are not made on this basis.
- Work is more safely retained; this is especially important for coursework.

These points still hold true. There may still be opposition from practitioners who believe that electronic written work is unacceptable, and there may be other practitioners who would like to have such ICT provision for their students but for whom it is not available. What we need to ensure, where we can, is that word-processing is readily accessible for class and school work and is not viewed as a treat.

Homework: Set homework at the start of the lesson

A Dyslexia-friendly approach to homework would include the ICT points above but could extend much further. Teachers could become more Dyslexia-friendly by setting homework at the start of the lesson, not at the end. This would make the link between class work and homework more apparent, giving students a chance to clarify their understanding and to note it down in legible format.

There is a continuing debate as to whether young students should be given homework. However, Directgov, the UK's public service website, provides a sliding scale suggesting how much time is recommended for homework, from one hour per week for years 1 and 2 (where children are 6 and 7 years old respectively) to two and a half hours per day in years 10 and 11 (where students are 15 and 16 years old). For younger children the website points out that 'homework' will involve reading to family members, but for dyslexic learners homework also means catching up on work not completed at school.

Many parents of dyslexic children are willing to help with homework but cannot read what has to be done from their child's writing, especially if the teacher calls this out at the last minute. Some schools operate homework helplines; paid-for, online support is also available.

However, homework misunderstandings can be avoided by thinking about what a dyslexic learner needs to know, and be able to access, in order to do the homework successfully.

Revision: Graphical representation

Many Dyslexia-friendly techniques and practices support revision because they do not depend on the written expression of an idea. Neil MacKay, the originator of the Dyslexia-friendly concept, notes that many of his recommended pedagogical activities were originally developed in order to support students undertaking examinations.

Though not everyone likes graphical representations, many students are helped to revise through using techniques such as the thought spray, spidergram or Buzan's Mind Map®. Each word in such a graphical representation is like a small iceberg, standing for a much larger area of knowledge. A graphical representation can be converted to a list by numbering the items.

Five steps in moving to all-through Dyslexia-friendly practice

Be well-informed about dyslexia.

↓

Adopt Dyslexia-friendly practices.

↓

Shape literacy work to target progress for individual dyslexic learners.

↓

Liaise with others – parents, professionals, policy-makers.

↓

Support the development of Dyslexia-friendly school policies.

Whole-school and whole-class strategies for a language and literacy focus

Recognising the importance of underlying language factors, Table 1.1 considers school and class strategies that support language development in relation to dyslexia.

Table 1.1 Whole-school and whole-class strategies for a language and literacy focus

	Early years	**Primary**	**Secondary**	**Tertiary**
Whole-school strategy	Policy and practice focus on language development.	School policy for literacy acquisition reflects Dyslexia-friendly methods.	The subject-focused curriculum allows for alternative ways of recording and demonstrating knowledge. All areas provide subject-specific vocabulary.	Strategy reflects possible late identification of dyslexia and makes arrangements and adjustments accordingly.
	There is a process for identifying speech and maturity or difficulty at school entry. There is access to speech and language advice.	There is a system in place for noticing and identifying readers and spellers who are falling behind and working with them.	There is a system for identifying signs of disaffection among poor readers. Where a child is showing behavioural difficulties, there is assessment for dyslexia and appropriate remediation.	All staff encourage the expression of sophisticated concepts and understanding. They appreciate how hard this may be for some dyslexic learners.
Whole-class strategy	Teaching encourages talking, speech sounds, rhyme, verbal interaction, story-telling, memory games.	Teaching encourages reading, spelling and written expression using Dyslexia-friendly approaches.	Teaching encourages written expression and subject knowledge, valuing an extended vocabulary even if it is not correctly spelled.	Teachers look for indicators that dyslexic learners are thinking faster than they can read or write, or that they are relying on old, unhelpful literacy habits.
	Teacher does not accept one-word answers and does not speak for a child. Teacher has access to speech and language advice for remediating language immaturities.	Classroom displays are clear and easy to read. They are not too chaotic or overcrowded.	Games and activities are developed to encourage confidence in using an extended vocabulary.	Teaching includes discussion with learners about how best they learn. Memory aids are used to help memorise subject-specific vocabulary.

Useful websites

These three major UK organisations provide information, advice and resources for practitioners, parents and people who experience dyslexia:

- The Dyslexia-SpLD Trust: http://www/thedyslexia-spldtrust.org.uk/
- British Dyslexia Association: http://www.bdadyslexia.org.uk/
- Dyslexia Action: http://www.dyslexiaaction.org.uk; their shop is at http://store.dyslexiaaction.org.uk

Further reading

MacKay, N. (2012) *Removing Dyslexia as a Barrier to Achievement* (3rd edn). Wakefield: SEN Marketing. Available from: http://www.senbooks.co.uk (email sales@senbooks.co.uk).

MacKay, N. and Tresman, S. (2005) *Achieving Dyslexia Friendly Schools Resource Pack*. London: British Dyslexia Association. Available online at: http://www.bdadyslexia.org.uk/ (training and accreditation section).

Rose, Sir J. (2009) *Identifying and Teaching Children and Young People with Dyslexia and Literacy Difficulties*. Nottingham: DCSF Publications.

2

Supporting learning

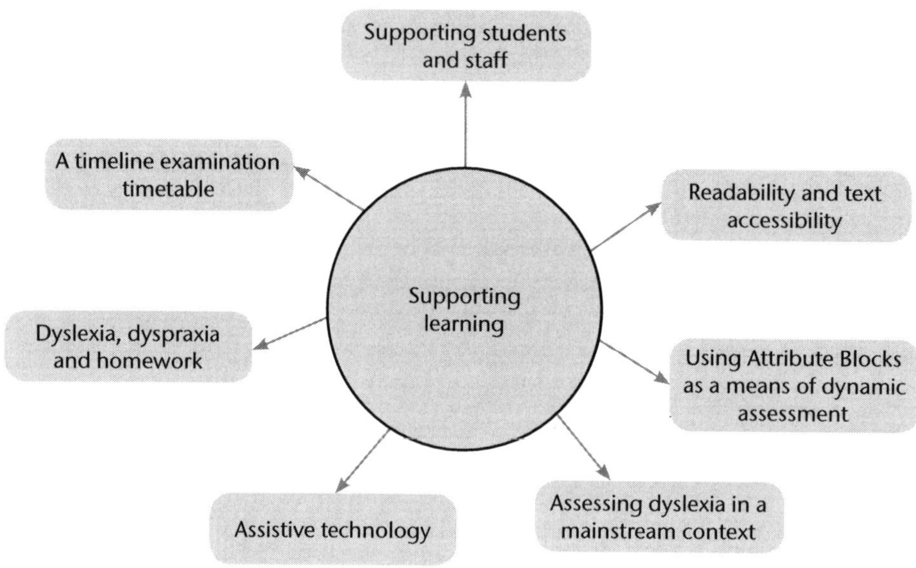

In a Dyslexia-friendly school good practice extends to everyone, not only to learners; disability legislation requires that no one is excluded from employment because of dyslexia and that reasonable adjustments should be made for staff as well as for students. Practitioners can be encouraged to show flair, sensitivity and skill towards dyslexic learners by being treated similarly themselves.

Good Practice Points: Supporting students and staff

Good practice points that are relevant equally for practitioners working with students and for managers training and advising staff are listed below. Our focus should be to:

1. Deal with the emotional aspects of literacy acquisition, specifically fear and lack of confidence. We can do this by adopting recognised Dyslexia-friendly practices and a 'can-do' attitude, demonstrating empathy, understanding and technique.

2. Employ Dyslexia-friendly practices in all interactions. This means using multi-sensory techniques, not relying on pen-and-paper tasks, finding alternative ways of recording and avoiding putting people 'on the spot' so they have time to collect and organise their thoughts.

3. Provide the 'big picture', the end-point, so that it is clear where work is heading and then use small steps to get there. Where there is incomplete understanding, we can put in a step, varying activities while reinforcing and rehearsing the teaching points.

4. Attach and relate new learning to learning that has gone before and is secure. We can acknowledge the impact of dyslexia by not necessarily expecting memory of what has gone before, but by gently encouraging its retrieval, perhaps through the use of memory techniques.

5. Discourage a discourse of deficit. We need not blame students for their literacy difficulties and we can refuse to accept or agree with a deficit view, whether it comes from children or adults. If necessary we can challenge this quite simply: it is society's high expectation of literacy that causes such difficulties for individuals who do not acquire it readily.

6. Use graphical and visual representations rather than large chunks of written prose to convey information. We can increase the power of representations by using different colours for different points made.

7. Encourage the use of questions. We can do this by giving reassurance that what is required is not to guess the answer that is in a teacher's or a trainer's head, but to open up genuine discussion.

8. Put pedagogical explanation in the hands of the teacher. We can do this by switching work around, so that teaching assistants can manage the rest of the class while a teacher focuses on learners who need extra explanation, instead of a teacher focusing on the majority of the class while teaching assistants work with learners who need help the most.

Readability and text accessibility

We can improve prose reading by making sure it is readable at a suitable level. Figure 2.1 is a photocopiable resource that shows how to check for readability in Microsoft Word 97–2003 documents, and in Word docx (Vista and Windows 7). A guide on how to make text resources as accessible as possible for readers can be found at section A of the Dyslexia-friendly Audit Tool (see Appendix).

There is a tool in these computer programs that can be used to improve the readability of text. First we must switch it on.

In **Word 97–2003** go to:

Tools

↓

Options

↓

Spelling and Grammar

↓

Check Readability statistics
(tick box to confirm)

In **Word 2007** and **Word docx**

Click on the Office button, at top left corner of a Word docx page

↓

Click on Word Options at the bottom of the menu shown

↓

In left menu, click on Proofing

↓

Tick the last box, 'Show readability statistics'

↓

Click OK

After this, we close this screen and type the text as a normal Word document. When we have finished, we run the spellchecker. On completion, the screen will display the readability statistics. We should:

- Aim for the lowest possible % of passive sentences.
- Aim for the lowest 'Flesch-Kincaid grade level' – this gives an American grade level.
- Aim for the highest possible measure of 'Flesch Reading Ease'.
- Add 5 to the Flesh-Kincaid level to get an approximate reading age.

Figure 2.1 Readability in Word 97–2003 and Word 2007 (Microsoft Vista) and Word docx (Microsoft Windows 7)

Something to Try: Using Attribute Blocks as a means of dynamic assessment

This resource is generally used in mathematics teaching to explore sets, linkages and pathways. In the activity below, a teacher who has concerns about any student's literacy can observe their listening and language skills, and their interactions, in a non-literacy task. Are they speedy, or do they need more time? Do friends try to help them? Do they forget part of the sequence of instructions, or do they have a particular strategy, such as using their fingers, to remember?

Students carrying out the activity sometimes demonstrate a significant difference between visual and verbal skills. This may trigger a teacher's closer consideration of how best that student might learn and record their knowledge, or it may indicate an area for concern. Without inclining toward diagnosis, this may cue a teacher to undertake closer observation or to put in place an intervention. In addition a teacher starting work with a literacy group of any age has the opportunity for a fun activity that does not trigger any apprehension that might be present. The activity provides a chance to explore thinking skills and to praise students outside of a literacy context, so building confidence.

1. First we explain that these are not toys or building blocks, they are equipment for practising thinking. (Attribute Blocks can be obtained through WY Educational Equipment Ltd.) We show the students that there are no two shapes the same – students will want to check this out for themselves. There are:
    - *three colours*
    - *two sizes*
    - *two thicknesses*
    - *five shapes.*

2. We ask individuals for specific shapes:
    - *'Haylie, please give me a large, thin, yellow triangle.'*
    - *This shows whether Haylie can carry four separate items of information or whether she consistently forgets one or two – it tells us something about Haylie's memory and about her sequencing skills.*
    - *Remind other students not to stare at the target!*

3. We begin a game of 'one different':
    - *Students work in a circle and make a chain of shapes, each one having 'one difference' from the shape before.*
    - *This may indicate whether there is anything affecting information processing, and/or memory, that would make a practitioner take note.*
    - *The difficulty can be increased to two differences, or three, or can be swapped to similarities, where students must find one characteristic the same.*
    - *Students can try to make the chain link together – this is rather unlikely, but it keeps the momentum of the activity.*

4. We praise students for their efforts:
    - *During the game, a teacher can tell students that s/he has noticed how well they are thinking and solving the problem.*
    - *A teacher can also tell students how well they are concentrating, and telling them this is what it means to concentrate – all eyes, ears and attention are on the task.*
    - *Afterwards, a teacher can ask students if they feel they have worked hard. They usually do feel this, because they have indeed worked hard concentrating and thinking, and solving the problem. A teacher can acknowledge the value of this cognitive activity, telling students that they are using their thinking well.*

5. We end by inviting students to make a picture with the shapes:
    - *This is not as easy as it sounds, since no two shapes are the same.*

- *The way students tackle this task says something about their skill in using visual materials, which may contrast with their literacy skills.*
- *A teacher can finish by asking students to sort the shapes back into the box. With the lid on, the box can be turned upside down to see if any fall out (the lid is usually reversed to keep the shapes in). Whether or not they fall, the session can end in laughter together, which engenders a positive attitude.*

Assessing dyslexia in a mainstream context

Dyslexia assessment has itself been subject to changes in dyslexia theory. The idea of a discrepancy between a student's literacy skills and their other achievements is always present, but we no longer measure the size of the gap between the actual and expected levels of literacy in order to identify dyslexia. Nor do we treat the characteristics of dyslexia as a checklist – dyslexia requires more subtlety of understanding than that. However, the gap between expected and actual literacy, between the level at which a child's peers are reading and/or spelling and the level at which a particular child is performing, remains at the heart of dyslexia assessment.

Dynamic assessment using informal methods and a teacher's professional skills provides the first level of assessment. A Dyslexia-friendly practitioner who is starting to monitor the progress of a student giving cause for concern, may then turn to standardised assessment procedures in order to support their request for further help, advice, materials or resources for a student. In addition, a practitioner may need evidence to put forward a request for an assessment by a specialist. The question then becomes one of whether, and where, a teacher can obtain test materials. We need to be careful, in case test materials have been kept too long and are now out of date. Reputable tests are revised to bring them up to date and it is always worth checking the date of publication.

Teacher-level assessments can be carried out in reading, spelling, handwriting, comprehension and mathematics. The assessment of reading can include phonological skills, whole word reading or group reading tests, non-word reading or the reading of words in context. Some tests indicate, on the score sheets, the levels at which the student becomes eligible for additional support or for special arrangements to be made in public examinations. The major test publishing companies have customer services advisers who are willing to discuss in detail the characteristics of their tests, so that teachers can choose suitably.

All reputable tests should have information about the size of the sample against which the tests were measured at the test design stage – a larger sample gives greater confidence than a small one. Teachers should seek information about the sample on which the instrument was tested and look for a recent date of publication. Teachers may also want to consider whether there are cultural differences in the test vocabulary, for instance between US and UK usage. Information about tests suitable for use by mainstream teachers in investigating the possibility of dyslexia is given at the end of this chapter.

Educators sometimes express concern that lack of success in school will lead to disaffection, leading in turn to truancy, anti-social behaviour and eventually crime. Dyslexia may be more highly represented in the prison population than in the population as a whole, but so too are other characteristics of special educational needs. There is not a direct causal relationship between dyslexia and crime; the links are much more subtle, and the impact of social disadvantage is also a factor. Equally, some older learners, particularly adults, may be relatively at ease with their dyslexia because they have other things about which they are confident, such as sporting, creative or entrepreneurial activity. The concept of pride in dyslexia is worth noting, as people celebrate the advantages that different ways of thinking, learning and doing can bring.

It is certainly true that emotional distress and anger can result from a sustained, negative school experience and this can be expressed in anti-social behaviour in school. Students always know who are the best readers and spellers in their class, and by definition who are the worst. The negative emotional impact of this ranking can be imagined, although different students will react in different ways. Some may keep a very low profile, relying on their friends to help them; others may react angrily and destructively. Some give up and withdraw from engaging with education, feeling increasingly isolated. If learners are behaving aggressively or rebelliously, it is always worth checking their literacy levels – if they will let us. Often they will be experiencing lower levels of literacy and some will be experiencing unidentified dyslexia.

Case Study: LeRoy

LeRoy shows dyslexic-type difficulties. In a literacy lesson his teacher asks a teaching assistant, Mrs A, to sit with his group, so that they may discuss their ideas for their own story, which is to be based on an existing, published story. The class are to use the framework of the story but introduce their own characters and events.

Mrs A has a lesson plan with objectives and learning outcomes on it so she is clear about the intended teaching points and outcomes. She focuses upon 'Fab vocab', as the class call it, writing notable words down on a whiteboard for the group to see, keeping the group on track. She also encourages LeRoy to take a full part and verbalise his story ideas for her to make notes.

Later in the lesson, Mrs A and LeRoy sit together with a story frame talking about his ideas and the collected 'fab vocab'. She helps LeRoy to make his own notes within the framework, encouraging him to check his work to make sure it makes sense. LeRoy has a wipe-clean laminated reminder card to use when he checks his work. It lists things to look out for: finger spaces, spelling, punctuation with some examples given to jog his memory, paragraphs and neat writing are all listed. His teacher has ticked the ones she wants him to think about when checking his notes. This helps him to remember he is writing notes rather than a polished piece of work.

Commentary: How might a Dyslexia-friendly teacher and school support LeRoy?

The case study shows a dyslexic learner being supported effectively in the classroom. Mrs A is being well-directed by her class teacher, and the lesson plan, which they may have worked out together, provides her with objectives and multisensory techniques to use. The activity is well designed to bring about the desired learning outcomes.

LeRoy may be a young child, perhaps just at the stages of early literacy, but the lesson would work just as well for an older student, and later in LeRoy's schooling, perhaps at around the age of 10, we might find similar activities taking place. However, we might also find the same lesson taking place when LeRoy is 13 years old or 15, if he has not made sufficient progress.

Meeting the needs of dyslexic students of any age frequently involves a tension between supporting a learner in the regular setting, creating a bridge to the curriculum for them, and alternatively withdrawing them, perhaps missing lessons, in order to provide them with a programme to advance their skills. The intention would be that new skills would transfer back into the regular curriculum, but this does not always happen as hoped. Transfer of skills may need a structured intervention of its own.

If a student does not make necessary progress, further intervention by way of a programme may be introduced, and the Dyslexia-SpLD Trust, in guidance to schools, makes the point that such a programme may need to be repeated. However, there are issues around how long a programme should be allowed to continue before being repeated or discarded. In this way time may pass; adolescents in this position, still finding themselves supported in the same way as described above, may need support for confidence, resilience and tolerance in addition to their literacy skills.

Student Voices: Kay

Here is the voice of Kay, now an educator and trainer herself, reflecting on her school experience:

> *What would have been fantastic, was if somebody could have helped me to understand myself, because I was furious and angry and my behaviour, to be fair to the teachers in the classroom, was terrible. If I could have understood that I wasn't stupid, to understand that dyslexia is real, there's a name for it, and that you can learn . . . I hated it, it was awful in school. They always used to say, on my school report, because the school reports were just disgusting, they just moaned and moaned how crap I was.* (Kay)

What might a Dyslexia-friendly teacher learn from this?

1. Kay's literacy difficulty is masked by her aggressive behaviour. It is likely that her teachers think that K's poor attitude is due to disaffection, a pure dislike of school and everything in it; there may be some truth in this. However, there is also the possibility of underlying difficulty.
2. The depth of feeling experienced by Kay is intense, even many years later in a successful adult life.
3. There is a need for a teacher to investigate, through assessment, the exact nature and scale of Kay's literacy difficulties, without being distracted by negative behaviour.
4. Kay is likely to need additional help with the gaining of literacy skills; she is struggling within regular classroom provision. This may have to be negotiated with Kay in order to be acceptable and manageable for her.
5. We expect greater understanding of literacy difficulty, now, than was perhaps the case when Kay was at school. A Dyslexia-friendly teacher understands the necessity of listening to a student and talking with them about how best to help them to learn.

Information and Communication Technology: Assistive technology

Following the Dyslexia-Friendly Schools pack, the British Dyslexia Association has produced a comprehensive ICT guide, updated in 2011 and authored by Victoria Crivelli. This can be found within the BDA website (via the Information and Activities page, in the Teachers and Schools menu).

The eight-page ICT supplement includes audit questions, features to look for when choosing software and software details. There is a detailed list of strategies, tools and programmes, matching ICT processes and practices with desired Dyslexia-friendly outcomes. The audit of ICT equipment and programmes available to support dyslexic learners in classrooms includes reading, writing, spelling and access opportunities. It covers the frequency and availability of ICT use in classrooms, including equipment to facilitate alternative forms of recording. A reading of this supplement provides a Dyslexia-friendly teacher with many ideas for using technology to help dyslexic learners of any age.

Homework: Dyspraxia advice

Dyspraxia is a term used to describe motor coordination problems which can involve both planning and execution (Kirby et al., 2010). In accordance with diagnostic criteria the condition may be called developmental coordination disorder (DCD). It may also be called developmental dyspraxia, and the term disorder of attention, movement and perception (DAMP) may be used in Scandinavian countries. Dyslexia may overlap with dyspraxia, as it may with other learning characteristics. Deponio (2004) summarises research literature suggesting that there is a noticeable overlap between dyslexia and dyspraxia in each direction. In broad terms, 40–50 per cent of dyslexic learners experience dyspraxia and similar proportions of dyspraxic learners experience dyslexia.

The Dyspraxia Foundation publishes a suite of classroom guidelines within its website, and Table 2.1 details the guidance offered regarding homework and the transfer of messages. This guidance is also highly relevant for dyslexia.

Revision: A timeline examination timetable

Sequencing, organisation and planning are aspects of learning that many students with dyslexia will experience as difficult, or even defeating. Ability to cope with the examination schedule can be aided by the production of a linear examination timetable, or timeline. This means showing the days one by one, on a larger scale and in a larger font. The timeline is produced on a length of paper which can be displayed fully on a classroom wall, or concertina'd to make a book. In this way the exam schedule, and opportunities for revision within it, can be more clearly identified (for example, see Figure 2.2).

Table 2.1 Dyspraxia foundation secondary classroom guidelines: homework and messages home – strategies for secondary school

Concern	Explanation	Strategies and accommodations
Homework isn't handed in	Individual hasn't written homework requirements down correctly. Forgets to hand homework in. Doesn't know where to hand homework in.	Give homework at the start of the lesson. Write homework requirements on a slip of paper for individual to stick into their planner. Put a sticker on planners to indicate people who need help to note their homework down. Write it in as you walk round the class. Collect the planners of people who need help at the start of the lesson and write homework down for them. Make sure the individual knows the system for handing in homework. Encourage form tutors to prompt individuals to hand in homework as part of a regular routine. Help the individual to set up a timetable to show when homework should be handed in. Work with parents to set up a system at home so the individual can plan ahead, particularly for project work. Before giving a detention for missing homework try to find out why homework hasn't been completed.
Homework is of a higher standard than class work	Individual is less distracted at home so finds it easier to focus. Parents provide support with planning and organisation of work.	Find out what support parents are providing at home – it is likely to be with the practical aspects of the task which allows the individual to concentrate on the content (*With dyslexia, it is likely to be support in literacy activities - authors*). Find out how much time an individual is spending on homework. Suggest suitable time limits.
Messages don't reach home	Individual loses pieces of paper. Forgets to hand papers to parents.	For important messages, contact parents directly. Help the individual to use their planner effectively. Encourage individuals to put messages and letters into a clear plastic wallet. Work with parents to use the planner as an effective means of communication.

Mon. 3rd	Tues. 4th	Wed. 5th	Thur. 6th	Fri. 7th	Week-end	Mon. 10th	Tues. 11th	Wed. 12th	Thur. 13th	Fri. 14th	Week-end
	Eng.		Sci. I	Biol.			Geog.		Lang.		
Music.		Math.				Hist.		Sci. II		ICT.	

Figure 2.2 Examination timetable expressed as a timeline

Five steps in moving to Dyslexia-friendly practice in supporting learning

Train all staff in Dyslexia-friendly practices.

↓

Train all staff by using Dyslexia-friendly practices.

↓

Schedule and protect planning time between teachers and teaching assistants.

↓

Encourage teachers to concentrate on learners with greatest need.

↓

Support dyslexic learners so that they learn in accordance with their ability level rather then their literacy level.

Whole-school and whole-class strategies for supporting learning

Table 2.2 considers school and class strategies that support learning in relation to dyslexia across the range of educational phases and stages. These are drawn from the literature, and particularly from the Ofsted reports *Reading by Six: How the Best Schools Do It* (2010) and *Removing the Barriers to Literacy* (2011).

Table 2.2 Whole-school and whole-class strategies for supporting learning

	Early years	**Primary**	**Secondary**	**Tertiary**
Whole-school strategy	Strategy expects clarity of objectives for literacy and pre-literacy skills. School gives training and examples. Objectives are not deficit-based.	School makes time available for teachers and teaching assistants to plan and consult together. This time is protected and does not rely on teaching assistants' goodwill in working beyond their paid hours in order to consult.	There is a champion for literacy, whose focus includes underachievement but also high achievement.	There is an awareness throughout that some students may have literacy difficulties and need departmental or general help, while others may have an identified specific learning difficulty such as dyslexia and are referred to student services.
	Support staff are trained to recognise early signs of reading difficulty.	Staff are trained to understand the structure of the phonics scheme in use.	Full use is made of data transfer at change of phase (primary to secondary). There are good relationships and good information exchange with 'feeder' secondary schools.	Academic staff use different forms of assessment in a module and together with student services consider alternative forms of assessment if necessary.
Whole-class strategy	Teachers and teaching assistants have the opportunity to agree how they will develop talking, listening, pre- and early literacy skills.	There is a focus on known underachieving groups, but support in class also includes highest achievers.	An objective for literacy is included in the planning for all subject areas.	Specialist tutors and notetakers support dyslexic students to help them to access the curriculum and express themselves appropriately for their course assessments.
	All staff use active listening and encourage questions from students. Staff use question and discussion to open up talk about the learning rather than close it down.	Pre-tutoring is used to prepare literacy work for the following week, focusing upon developing and using phonics skills needed in the work.	Teaching assistants (TAs) are not left to work with students who find learning hardest. When there is a need for intensifying input, teachers switch with TAs. TAs can then oversee the majority, and teachers can give more detailed teaching to learners who need it.	Tutors recognise different, original thinking that is not dependent upon literacy skills. They allow scope in the curriculum and in assessment for thinking of this kind.

Useful websites

- Dyspraxia Foundation: http://www.dyspraxiafoundation.org.uk
- SpLD Assessment Standards Committees: http://www.sasc.org.uk
- WY Education Equipment Ltd: http://www.wyedu.co.uk/

Assessment materials

Many of the educational tests purchased in the UK come from the following providers:

- GL Assessment: http://www.gl-assessment.co.uk
- Hodder: http://www.hoddertests.co.uk/
- Pearson: http://www.pearsonclinical.co.uk/

A list of tests approved for use in the identification of dyslexia can be found at the website for the SpLD Assessment Standards Committee (SASC); in the right-hand-side menu, go to SpLD testing and assessment guidance 2012. Not all of these can be used by mainstream teachers as some require a specialist educator's training or a psychology degree.

Further reading

Office for Standards in Education (Ofsted) (2010) *Reading by Six: How the Best Schools do It.* Manchester: Ofsted. Available online at: http://www.ofsted.gov.uk.

Office for Standards in Education (Ofsted) (2011) *Removing Barriers to Literacy.* Manchester: Ofsted. Available on-line at http://www.ofsted.gov.uk.

Blatchford, P., Bassett, P., Brown, P., Martin, C., Russell, A. and Webster, R. (2009) *Deployment and Impact of Support Staff Project.* (DCSF-RB148). London, Department for Children, Schools and Families.

3

Dyslexia and phonics

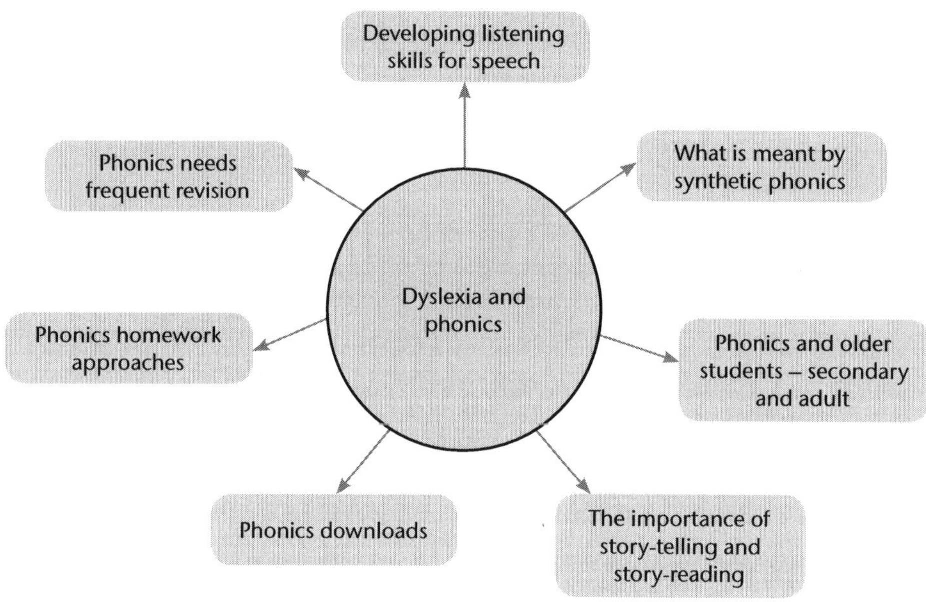

Increasing interest in the underpinning skills and concepts involved in language relates to the identification of dyslexia as a difficulty associated, although not exclusively, with reduced activation in the areas of the brain concerned with speech and language. Recent years have seen the development of new interests in talking and listening projects to develop speech, language and comprehension, such as the Talk for Learning project carried out in North Yorkshire (Alexander, 2003; Smit, n.d.); and the Talking Time project in Tower Hamlets (Dockrell and Stuart, 2007). Staff training may be necessary to draw attention to the importance of talking for learning, in the face of the pressures created by other curriculum demands.

Good Practice Points: Developing listening skills for speech

Sometimes students enter education with undeveloped skills for distinguishing spoken sounds. Teachers need to make sure that:

1. Adults model listening to children, telling them what they are doing and how (note that 'how' is not the same as 'why').
2. Children are given reasons to listen.
3. Sound games, listening games, stories, rhymes, songs, musical sounds are used.
4. Adults name interesting sounds in the environment.
5. Children are listened to by adults who model good listening skills and who point out what these are.
6. Children are taught that they need to look at the face or mouth of the one who is talking.
7. Children unused to listening or reluctant to listen to each other are reoriented and praised to secure this as routine.
8. Information is requested about any hearing problems or recurrent ear infections.
9. If concerns persist, parents and SEN specialists are consulted about arranging a hearing test.

Figure 3.1 provides a photocopiable guide to early literacy, describing first stages in gaining phonics knowledge and awareness, although teachers of older learners may also find this of relevance.

What is meant by synthetic phonics?

Since phonological difficulty is frequently found as a characteristic of dyslexia, a systematic phonics approach is considered to be particularly valuable for dyslexic learners. As a result of government policy, children in UK schools are taught the sounds (*phonemes*) which make up the building blocks of phonetically correct words. From nursery level children are taught how to listen for sounds and to blend or synthesise them to hear words, hence the term *synthetic phonics*.

The English alphabet contains 26 different letters, making 25 different sounds (C and K making the same sound); however there are more sounds than these. A synthetic phonics approach recognises almost double the number of sounds into which words can be *blended and segmented* to read or spell phonetically correct words. The number of these additional graphemes/phonemes varies from scheme to scheme, although 44 is often quoted. It is important to understand the difference that using *phonemes* makes to being able to read easily. Sounding out the phonemes v/e/s/t will make the word 'vest', whereas using the names of the letters vee/ee/ess/tee clearly does not help.

The most thorough published schemes also include *graphemes* which can be read in different ways, for example 'oo' differs in 'look' and 'boot', while 'ow' differs in 'snow' and 'cow'. Through carefully structured programmes, students are taught how to use their knowledge of letter patterns within words to *re-code*, that is to translate phonemes to graphemes, and vice versa. In most cases children are then able to read, correctly, words which may not even

<table>
<tr><th>Teaching input</th><th>Developing phonics knowledge and awareness</th><th>Good practice points</th></tr>
<tr><td rowspan="5">Talking for learning</td><td>Children begin to talk to each other in their play.</td><td>Children are praised for talking to each other, especially when extended sentence structures are used.</td></tr>
<tr><td rowspan="4">Children learn to enjoy books and stories.</td><td>Children are told and retold stories, and are read and reread story books.</td></tr>
<tr><td>Children have access to a range of interesting high-quality books to read or share in their own time. Some are dual language books.</td></tr>
<tr><td>Children have comfortable places to enjoy reading and sharing books with adults and friends.</td></tr>
<tr><td>Children can retell familiar and cultural stories, and attempt to sound out words, copying 'being the teacher'.</td></tr>
<tr><td rowspan="2">Letter sounds</td><td>Initial letter sounds.</td><td>As soon as children are able to sit with a group and listen, a gentle introduction to letter sounds can be made. Sounds are introduced in line with the school's chosen scheme.</td></tr>
<tr><td>Parents and carers as partners.</td><td>Schools encourage parents, carers and families to support children's phonics work, by showing them teaching strategies and materials used in class, plus correct pronunciation of sounds and accompanying actions.</td></tr>
</table>

Figure 3.1 A guide to developing early literacy

be part of their spoken vocabulary. Words such as 'flare', 'throng' and later 'scintillate' are decodable using the synthetic phonics approach once phonemes are mastered.

The English language contains many irregular or complex words; about 85 per cent are words which can be broken down easily into their component sounds while 15 per cent cannot[1]. The number of words one can break down into sounds depends on the number of phonemes one recognises. A 4-year-old child who recognises 've' as making the 'v' sound will be able to read 'have' as h/a/ve. Someone who does not know this will see this word as a 'tricky' or irregular word.

Phonics and older learners

Secondary level students

In *Removing Barriers to Literacy* (Ofsted, 2011), inspectors address the issue of the lack of systematic phonics teaching at secondary level. They recommend that all learners without appropriate phonics knowledge should receive suitable teaching and that all practitioners should receive regular and updated training in literacy. In the USA the term Response To Intervention (RTI) is used to discuss the special educational needs of learners but without employing a discourse of deficit; students who have difficulties in making progress may be described as non-responders or minimal responders. The idea of intervention also reflects a general view that literacy work is the responsibility of specialists who may administer a phonics programme rather than of subject teachers. While all sources acknowledge that some students will need a more intensified specialist intervention, it is within the mainstream context that Ofsted seeks to extend literacy knowledge to the wider range of practitioners.

The inclusion of a literacy target within subject teachers' planning, as Ofsted suggests, raises questions about what these targets should be like in order to be Dyslexia-friendly. There is little research available to discuss how the teaching of phonics might take place in mainstream secondary education within the remit of subject teachers. However, Karen Edwards undertook an intervention programme that involved supporting and working with a mainstream English teacher to develop literacy work within the subject. Edwards carried out a miscue analysis among struggling readers aged 14–16 identifying the areas in which they were weak. The intervention then taught the missing knowledge. While this research did not focus upon dyslexia, it is of interest through its use of miscue analysis and through its outcomes. Edwards found students missing knowledge in these areas:

- how to read the word endings /ance/, /ine/, /ion/, /ous/, /ious/, /que/, /ence/, /ment/;
- whether to read the letters c and g as a short ('hard') or a long ('soft') vowel;
- vowel combinations /ai/, /ay/, /au/, /aw/, /augh/, /ei/, /eigh/, /ey/, /eu/, /ew/, /eau/, /ea/, /ie/, /y/, /oo/, /oe/, /oi/, /oy/, /ou/, /ow/, /ough/, /ui/, /ue;
- consonant blends ('teams').

(Edwards, 2008: 549)

Knowing that these would be areas of vulnerability in student literacy, a subject teacher at secondary level could intensify teaching of any of these combinations as they arose in new vocabulary. Secondary teachers could also focus on how to develop the learning of new

[1]Reid 2009; 175 citing Cox, 1985.

spellings. A traditional spelling test will not help dyslexic learners; a short spelling test with five or fewer words might be more helpful. The literature suggests that all students benefit from such input, not only learners who struggle with literacy.

In considering how secondary subject teachers can act on the need for literacy input, Reed et al. (2012) note that teachers will need to be supported by resources and by management and administration in the form of staff training and monitoring of practice. Practitioners can develop their practice by creating:

- Ways for teachers to classify words into content-specific, academic and common words.
- Routines to help students break multi-syllable words apart by syllables and/or morphemes (prefixes, roots and suffixes).
- Opportunities to explore examples and non-examples of words being used in different contexts.
- Opportunities to compare and contrast related words.

(Reed et al., 2012: 44)

The authors point out that embedding vocabulary, spelling and comprehension work into subjects will not be sufficient, of itself, to help readers who have literacy difficulties. Nevertheless they agree that these areas provide a useful place to start.

Adult students

> *My university tutor asked me if I thought I might be dyslexic. I had joked for years that I was, but for her to ask me, it took a long time for me to come to terms with. So many missed opportunities . . .* (Jane aged 27)

At the adult level the need for the development of literacy skills, including phonics, has been recognised for some time. It has been manifested in adult literacy programmes and in meeting the UK Equality Duty through adjustments made to support mature learners.

Adults who experience dyslexia may have developed strategies to enable them to read well enough to do all that is necessary for their work or lifestyle. They may have found work involving little or no reading, or may have studied subjects which may be more mathematical and so require less reading or writing. Reading will probably be slower for them than for their peers, and it may lack automaticity and fluency. Some adults go out of their way to hide their difficulties, for example by saying that they have forgotten their glasses so as not to be required to read.

Sometimes, mature adults refer themselves for diagnostic assessment or seek adult literacy classes because they cannot read bedtime stories to their children easily, and this is felt most keenly. Reduced literacy may have an emotional impact upon parents, particularly if their children can read or spell better than themselves.

While adults may come to read single words easily, a block of text can be exhausting or daunting to read. When reading aloud, fluency can be lost and many substitutions and omissions can occur which may not change the text greatly, but which give a lower level of accuracy. They may also miss words at the ends of lines or small connective words such as 'it', 'was', 'or'. A lower level of reading accuracy may be accompanied by lower levels of phonological awareness.

When working with an adult, it is important to explore the individual's experience and discover when difficulties started to affect them, how they experience literacy now and the strategies they may have developed to cope with this. It is necessary to progress with sensitivity. A diagnosis of possible dyslexia, no matter how likely the adult feels it may be, can be traumatic.

An adult's reading has to be assessed, formally or informally, to explore their reading skill level. It is important to explain the process of reading and to focus, in the first instance, on words that are already recognised and known. A systematic, phonics-based reading programme might be suggested. This can be very effective, allowing the individual to proceed at their own pace. A tutor will check that the student has fluency and understanding at one level before proceeding to the next. We aim to concentrate on meaning in reading and the derivation of the words. Showing the adult how to recognise the root word will help with spelling in particular.

Depending on the literacy level of an adult student, a highly structured, systematic, multisensory phonics programme can be really helpful. Whether this is accepted by an older learner and how this is given will depend on the age, personality and experience of our student. Further and higher education establishments have staff trained ready to support learners who experience, or may experience, dyslexia. Students are encouraged to talk to them to discover what can be offered by way of support and guidance.

Something to Try: Using story-telling and story-reading to aid the teaching of phonics

To be able to learn phonics children must be able to focus their attention on an adult. A good way to ensure they can do this is to tell or read stories to groups of children at a set time each day. Through story-telling and story-reading children learn to sit together quietly as a group, to concentrate on what the adult has to share with them and to listen to their teacher for a period of time.

The practice of retelling or rereading the same story for a number of days will encourage children to engage with the story through familiarity. The developing engagement will support children in learning that print carries meaning and remains the same over a period of days, that pictures and words represent real things such as houses, animals and people. Later, children become aware of settings and characters real or imagined. Most importantly, story-telling and story-reading introduces children to a wealth of new vocabulary which they might otherwise never encounter. Such vocabulary is introduced in context.

To support the acquisition of new words, it is important for children to hear the same story for a number of days in succession. The teacher can now introduce a powerful tool for blending sounds into words. In a story about the red hen – this is a traditional tale, retold by many authors, but see for example Zamach (1979) – the teacher may break the flow of the story at the word *hen* and sound it out: 'Then I will do it myself, said the little red h/e/n/' and teacher immediately gives the blended word which the children already know to be hen.

The children know the word to be *hen* having heard the story read to them regularly. This technique can be implemented with any phonically regular word, e.g. d/o/g, ch/i/p, f/l/air, b/u/tt/er, etc. The statement of the whole world coming immediately after sounding-out increases the chance of remembering. Children who hear words being segmented and blended in quick succession are more confident when the time comes for them to do so themselves in a more structured session.

Case study: Jodie

There are times when a familial dyslexia link is clear, and then perhaps both child and parent can be helped.

Jodie was a shy, quiet child who lived with her extended family. She was struggling with her phonics learning, and her teacher was wondering whether she might be experiencing a specific learning difficulty in literacy. Jodie's teacher had never met her father until one day after school Jodie was collected by a man she proudly told her teacher was her dad. A couple of days later Jodie's father asked to talk to the teacher regarding Jodie's homework. The three of them went back into the classroom where Jodie's dad explained that he had been away for a long time and had missed out on Jodie's formative years. He was now determined to change his life and make sure Jodie had a better start in life than he had experienced.

Jodie's father told the teacher that his own reading skills were very poor and he felt he was unable to help Jodie as he would like to do. He was worried as he genuinely wished to support her. The teacher asked Jodie to show her father how she did phonics in school each day. Jodie sat close to her dad as she showed him the flash cards one by one, sounding each out. The teacher gave them a tick sheet to complete each time they did the homework. She encouraged Jodie's father to come in to chat whenever he needed to.

That was the last time she saw Jodie's father until parents' evening weeks later. He came in to the room with a broad smile and explained that he was astonished with the progress Jodie was making and overjoyed that they were learning to read together. He felt that he understood his own reading and spelling so much better that his self-esteem had grown enough to seek adult literacy classes.

Commentary: How might a Dyslexia-friendly teacher and school support Jodie?

This would have been an unexpected circumstance for Jodie's teacher. Preparing to discuss Jodie's literacy difficulties, she finds herself discussing Jodie's father's literacy problems, and needing to do so in a non-judgemental way. Understanding that dyslexia has a notable level of heritability Jodie's teacher may not be surprised, but she may need to remember that it will have required a great deal of confidence for Jodie's father to speak out. In the event she deals with the challenge very well, arranging activities so that both Jodie and her father can benefit. In due course there are literacy results for both.

Parents who struggled to learn to read, for whatever reason, have a second chance as their child brings home phonics homework. It is worth remembering that many may not have been taught phonics at all. As with Jodie's father above, daily practice with their child may improve their own understanding and confidence. In addition every school should know where local adult literacy classes can be found – a Dyslexia-friendly school can display this information in an accessible way, without parents having to seek it out.

Student Voices: Sophie

Here are the words of Sophie, whose teachers are concerned about her falling behind in reading and spelling:

> *The teacher tells me what we are going to do next and I understand, but when I stand up I can only remember bits like I need crayons or to sit with the blue group.* (Sophie age 7)

What might a Dyslexia-friendly teacher learn from this?

1. Links between poor memory and dyslexia are well established. If s/he has not already done so, Sophie's teacher needs to consider the possibility of dyslexia. Rather than criticising or reprimanding, Sophie's teacher needs to find ways of helping her to remember instructions.

2. Ways for her teacher to help Sophie to remember might include:
   - keeping instructions to a minimum;
   - reducing background distractions when giving instructions;
   - giving instructions twice (once to focus attention, then once more to get the meaning across);
   - using other means than speaking in order to convey them;
   - asking for instructions to be repeated back;
   - teaching Sophie to rehearse instructions to herself.

3. Her teacher needs to take note of whether Sophie shows signs of an information-processing or speech-processing problem of any kind.

4. Her teacher needs to take note of whether there are recognisable dyslexic characteristics present in Sophie's work – s/he has already noted a delay in reading and spelling progress.

5. If concerns continue, Sophie's teacher needs to alert the school's SEN Coordinator or a specialist teacher, and ask for further advice.

Information and Communication Technology: Phonics practice and the Internet

There is a wide range of websites and smart-phone applications (apps) available for children to download and use themselves at little or no cost. Some are designed to be used alongside the phonics schemes employed in schools while others are used alone. There are also clips of teachers teaching interesting and fun phonics lessons, available free on YouTube. Children can choose from among these to reinforce their knowledge and skills in an engaging and motivating way.

Where an app or website has been carefully selected the extra exposure to phonics, spelling or reading tasks, in a non threatening and fun way, can only help. However, we need to be aware of 'screen clutter'. For students with dyslexia, the less there is on a screen the easier it is for them to focus their attention correctly. If a child displays dyslexic tendencies, then differing accents for letter names and sounds may lead to unwelcome confusion and a slowing down of learning in school. Cluttered screens with moving items can prove distracting or tiring even to adults with dyslexia. If parents are in doubt about the suitability of an app or website, a child's teacher should be able to advise. Some useful websites for phonics practice are shown at the end of this chapter.

Homework: Phonics study at home, guided by school

Students who show or are at risk of developing dyslexic tendencies will make better progress with regular, short spells of homework to reinforce each day's learning. To maximise this learning opportunity, many schools offer parents a workshop-type open meeting. At this meeting it is usual to tell parents the background philosophy of the school's chosen phonics scheme, its extent and coverage, its teaching and learning style and the best way parents can support their child at home.

Some schemes depend on follow-up at home to reinforce teaching points; others make no mention of it. Some schemes are stand-alone programmes focusing on basic phonic letter-learning and spelling; others offer handwriting and letter formation strategies. The best programmes build on this and progress into highly structured, integral reading and spelling schemes.

It is the responsibility of each school to guide their families. It is vital, whatever else is desired, that families are given a very clear understanding of how to pronounce each sound; the essential point is the correct pronunciation of pure sounds. A pure sound is the target sound alone without the unconscious addition of an 'ugh' on the end. Thus 'sssss' is the long pure sound as opposed to 'suhhh' and 'b' is a short clipped sound bouncing from the lips as opposed to 'buhhh'.

The second key aspect to share with families is the difference between the names and sounds of letters. Some families will have forgotten how they learned to read and spell, others will have been taught to do so using names of letters alone and others might remember 'baby names' for letters. Parents will need to be shown, or reminded, that to build a word from its component parts we will need the sounds rather than the names in order to hear correctly what the word is or how it might be spelt.

Revision: Phonics revision needs to be frequent

Phonics revision probably needs to take place on a daily basis, even when a learner develops maturity. The reason for this is the increased stimulation that is needed in order for the learning to be retained. Major dyslexia specialist programmes for systematic phonics often use a procedure incorporating cards or other practical materials which are to be rehearsed on a daily basis.

However, it is sometimes difficult for dyslexic learners to find the enthusiasm to do regular practice, and it is also hard for parents to insist in the face of opposition. Nevertheless, students who display dyslexic tendencies will require very much more revision, repetition and rehearsing of knowledge and skills before they are retained in the long-term. This reflects the difficulties with phoneme-grapheme transition, memory and sequencing that are found in the experience of dyslexia.

Five steps in moving to Dyslexia-friendly phonics practices

Use telling/reading of stories and talking with adults to develop listening skills, vocabulary and the purposeful nature of speech and print.

↓

Link consistent actions with phonic sounds to jog memory.

↓

Offer remedial support as soon as a child starts to fall behind their peers.

↓

Remember that school work is very tiring to dyslexic learners – revise, revisit, rehearse and rest.

↓

Phonics work may need to continue for longer, including regular rehearsal, than might otherwise be expected in literacy learning.

Whole-school and whole-class strategies for dyslexia and phonics

Table 3.1 considers school and class strategies that support the development of phonics skills and awareness across the range of educational phases and stages.

Table 3.1 Whole-school and whole-class strategies for dyslexia and phonics

	Early years	**Primary**	**Secondary**	**Tertiary**
Whole-school strategy	There is a whole-school approach to teaching phonics. This includes inter-class moderation of phonics lessons to ensure consistency.	School policy for phonic acquisition reflects multisensory, Dyslexia-friendly methods.	School continues to build phonics skills where necessary. Age/stage-appropriate phonic teaching approaches and materials are available.	Strategy is to promote continued work on systematic phonics while understanding that students' primary desire may be to understand and complete their scholastic work.
	Phonic teaching begins in Nursery or age 3 where children learn to listen and identify sounds in their environment, leading to letter sound correlation.	There is a system in place for noticing and identifying learners who have difficulty with phonics, and assessing/working with them at the earliest point.	Schools are able to revitalise this learning through sensitive use of schemes and tuition – not just giving more of the same work at which a learner has already failed.	This policy is made clear through published objectives, learning contracts and service level agreements. Where students experience dyslexia, the expectation is that part of support sessions will include the building of literacy skills.
Whole-class strategy	Nursery rhymes are taught and sung daily. Children are encouraged to identify rhymes in stories.	Phonic sounds practice is woven into every aspect of early school life.	Lesson objectives are made clear to students.	Student support sessions include phonics-based building of literacy skills.
	Children see adults writing for a purpose regularly. Families are encouraged to learn the phonics teaching process.	Individual progress is monitored.[1]	ICT is used to support wherever possible when the need for handwriting is not the objective of a lesson.	Five- or ten-minute activities are developed to work on aspects of phonics skills. Objectives are set in discussion with students. The tone is kept light and enjoyable, adult to adult.

[1]An intervention or programme is in place when literacy delay is evident.

Useful websites

Free phonics-based activities and games are available from:

- Joined Up Resources: http://www.familylearning.org.uk and http://www.letter-and-sounds.com/
- Kent Children's Trust, Kent County Council (2012) 'Kent ICT Literacy CLL games' (author James Barratt): http://www.kenttrustweb.org.uk/kentict/content/games/literacy.htm
- Phonics for Adult Literacy (author Tricia Millar): http://www.phonics-for-adult-literacy.com/uploads-downloads/

Further reading

Bald, J. (2007) *Using Phonics to Teach Reading and Spelling*. London: SAGE.

Lloyd, S. M. (2001) *The Phonics Handbook: A Handbook for Teaching Reading, Writing and Spelling (Jolly Phonics)*. Chigwell: Jolly Learning Ltd.

Rose, Sir J. (2006) *Independent Review of the Teaching of Early Reading*. Nottingham: Department for Education and Skills.

4

Dyslexia and English as an additional language

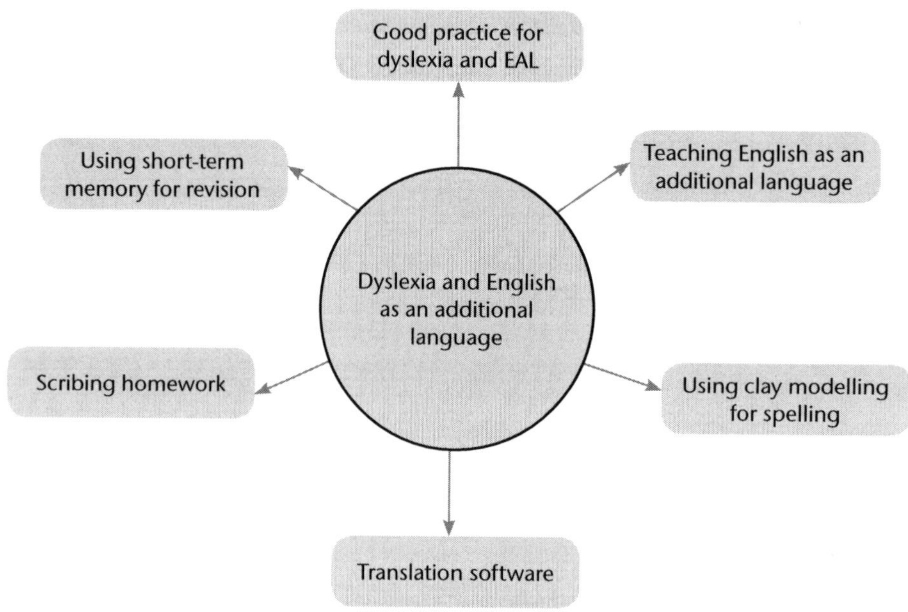

It is generally accepted that about 10 per cent of people experience dyslexia and of these about 4 per cent experience it in a significant way. This means that in classes averaging 30 pupils and with a non-selective intake there will be at least one child who experiences notable dyslexia, and a few more whose need is not so great but who may be finding literacy difficult. If dyslexia is part of a range of literacy acquisition, it follows, statistically, that some learners for whom English is not the first language will also experience dyslexia. Where English is an additional language, dyslexia may be masked by other language or social factors.

Good Practice Points: Students with possible dyslexia who have English as an additional language

In order to help a learner of English who might be experiencing dyslexia, we need to:

1. Consider the emotional impact, allowing longer time for accommodating to a new language.
2. Create a supportive multilingual environment, respecting other languages and cultures. We can do this by applying Dyslexia-friendly resource techniques (see Appendix 1) to multilingual displays and wordings.
3. Always consider dyslexia if a child is struggling with literacy; we should not assume it is a consequence of using more than one language.
4. Be aware that dyslexia in a different language or orthography may manifest itself differently.
5. Enquire whether our student struggles in literacy in their home language.
6. Liaise with the EAL specialist in the use of informal and formal assessments.
7. Use Dyslexia-friendly programmes, resources and differentiation.
8. Build students' phonics knowledge and phonics awareness, but use words and morphemes also, as these may be easier for a dyslexic learner to hear and to master.
9. Ensure that new learning is connected to earlier learning. We should not seek to adopt a 'sticking plaster' approach, where miscellaneous worksheets and activities are employed to fill a learning gap. With dyslexia, this new learning may not be retained.
10. Build up reading speed and fluency. We can do this by focusing on naming speed, word recognition and automaticity. We can support students setting their own targets of a number of words read (or written) in a minute.
11. Understand that literacy progress in one language will transfer to progress in another and choose one language as the focus for this work to avoid confusion. But also:
12. Seek specialist advice about teaching languages separately or together.
13. Make sure any dictation or copying from the board is restricted to a very few lines and allow extra time.
14. Use story-telling and retelling involving oral, visual and action communication.
15. Involve parents in story-telling, in making dual language books and materials, and in cultural celebrations.
16. Create support materials tailored to the individual learner – helping our student also helps other learners. We build a resource bank, and show parents that we are focusing upon their child.
17. Provide opportunities for structured literacy learning activities to carry on for longer.
18. Consider the realignment of existing language programmes (Schneider, 2009) to reflect small-step, systematic, cumulative learning of phonological, morphemic and word elements.
19. Seat a dyslexic learner nearer to the front – not right at the front, because s/he may need to see what others are doing, and also to share, collaborate and initiate work and play activities.
20. Make ICT readily available for classroom work, but allow our student to write by hand if they prefer.

Reed et al. (2012: 47) provide a Fidelity Tool for embedded reading instruction, whereby one practitioner can audit the practice of another, judging the quality of intervention according to identified standards. We offer the above Good Practice Points as an informal Fidelity Tool (see Figure 4.1), suggesting that practitioners complete it with a colleague annually. This provides an opportunity to think through and communicate good practice by focusing on examples and by setting a priority target for the next evaluation period.

Good Practice Points	Do I do this? Y/N/Sometimes	If yes, example/evidence
Consider emotional impact, allowing longer time for a new language		
Create a supportive multilingual environment		
Always consider dyslexia if a child is struggling with literacy		
Be aware that dyslexia in a different language may show itself differently		
Enquire whether our student struggles in literacy in their home language		
Liaise with the EAL specialist regarding assessment of literacy		
Use Dyslexia-friendly programmes, resources and differentiation		
Build students' phonics knowledge and phonics awareness, using words and morphemes also		
Ensure that new learning is connected to earlier learning		
Build up reading speed and fluency in multilingual learners		
Choose one language as the focus for this work		
Seek specialist advice about teaching languages separately or together		
Limit any dictation or copying from the board and allow extra time		
Use story-telling and retelling involving oral, visual and action		
Involve parents in story-telling, making dual language books and materials, and in cultural celebrations		
Create support materials tailored to the individual learner		
Provide opportunities for literacy learning activities to carry on for longer		
Consider the realignment of existing language programmes to support dyslexia learning needs		
Seat a dyslexic learner nearer to the front (not right at the front)		
Make ICT readily available for classroom work, allowing student to write by hand if they prefer		

The next priority target for good practice in Dyslexia+EAL ....

....

Anything else to mention?..

Date......................... Signed: (1) Practitioner......................... (2) Auditor..

Figure 4.1 A good practice fidelity tool for teaching students with possible dyslexia who have English as an additional language

Teaching English as an additional language

There are different ways of thinking about teaching English as an additional language, including the teaching of English in global contexts. Ferguson (2006: 8) discusses the 'massive popular demand for English skills', as a growing international trend, and some societies, for example Wales, use dual languages, one of which is English.

Within the requirement of teaching English to multilingual children, Wyse and Jones (2008) make the point that:

> The least successful way to deliver English teaching to a multilingual child with a poor grounding in English is to remove them from the classroom setting and provide short sharp bursts of tuition in isolation. (Wyse and Jones, 2008: 250)

Overington (2012) confirms that while this can still take place in order to build skills quickly, most teaching of multilingual children takes place in regular classrooms, with an emphasis upon gaining English literacy skills as quickly as possible. There is a similarity here with early dyslexia teaching that used withdrawal as the predominant tuition method, whereas now there is much more interest in helping students with dyslexia in the mainstream classroom. A lesson from dyslexia experience is that learning literacy 'as quickly as possible' may not always be feasible and that adjustments have to be made.

Since multilingualism is increasing, this too may benefit from a Dyslexia-friendly approach. This is considered to be good for all children, and Wyse and Jones suggest that a multisensory focus is likewise of benefit to multilingual students. There is a kinship between Dyslexia-friendly techniques and multilingual techniques that suggests that a Dyslexia-friendly approach can be fruitful; if a multilingual learner experiences dyslexia, Dyslexia-friendly techniques will offer both language and literacy support. The checklist for accessibility of resources included as part A in the Audit Tool (see Appendix 1) will also help students for whom English is not the first language, and might be considered essential for learners who experience both learning characteristics.

Something to Try: Using clay modelling to develop literacy skills

The Davis method® is registered and embodied in the Davis® training programme entitled 'Symbol Mastery'. Examples of use of the Davis® clay modelling technique have appeared in the literature in the context of teaching and learning a second language. Ambrose and Loh (2011) report positive results in dyslexic Malaysian students' learning of English using this programme (although a control group was not used), and Serrano-Lopez and Poehner (2008) report the beneficial use of clay modeling in English students' learning of Spanish prepositions.

While acknowledging that the method is part of a structured programme, experience shows that when the technique is used, two further benefits can occur. The first is that when a student, under a teacher's direction, is following the method to learn a spelling, those around may also learn it at the same time. This means that the technique can be a group activity. The second benefit is that, after working with clay modelling, sometimes we do not actually need the clay – asking someone 'what would you model to help you remember . . .' can get results too.

The clay modelling technique works as follows:

1. First we need the correct spelling available.
2. We go through the word with the learner, finding out which part causes difficulty – do they know how the word starts, and how it ends? Discussion of this type usually reveals some sticking point –for example the 'double r' in the word diarrhoea, or the order of vowels in the name 'Phoebe', or the suffix 'ation'.
3. Once the point of difficulty has been identified, we ask our student to think of something they could model that would help them remember that part, correctly spelled.
4. We take care not to make suggestions or to criticise the modelling; the point is that it is meaningful to our student.
5. We allow time for the modelling to take place – during this time a student is thinking about the correct spelling of the word!
6. Finally we ask our student to construct the word out of clay 'worms' and display it in front of the model.

Although this method makes a vivid and meaningful impact, to secure the word it is advisable to rehearse it from time to time, recalling both our hand-made model and our spelling. Capturing these in a photo could be helpful.

Identifying Dyslexia when English is an additional language

A Dyslexia-friendly teacher is likely to notice children who are not making sufficient literacy progress over time, whose rate of progress is slow and who may be avoiding or becoming distressed over literacy tasks. S/he may notice memory, sequencing or organising difficulties, and may contrast these with a student's strengths in areas that do not depend on literacy. Where a teacher has access to an EAL support teacher, this specialist will be able to discuss whether a child is experiencing an unexpected level of difficulty with gaining literacy in their home language, in addition to English. This would be a useful indicator of an underlying difficulty.

Once alerted, it is possible to carry out informal assessments such as observation, discussion, miscue analysis, reading tests and spelling tests, handwriting and dictation. These can be managed sensitively so that the student is not vulnerable to embarrassment because of low scores. A teacher may also notice whether a learner relies on the support of friends in literacy work, or whether poor behaviour coincides with literacy lessons and tasks, with the understanding that these might be indicators of learning distress.

Assessment instruments for dyslexia tend to be standardised on native English speakers. However, a teacher seeking a more formal assessment instrument may consider Frederickson et al. (1997), who investigated the validity of their Phonological Assessment Battery (PhAB) with a small group of bilingual students who were home speakers of Bengali/Sylheti, but who were also fluent in English. While recommending caution because of the small sample size (50 children), the authors concluded that:

> PhAB appears to be an appropriate tool for identifying bilingual children who are experiencing difficulties of a phonological nature. (Frederickson et al., 1997)

Children in Wales can be assessed in Welsh or English although few tests are available in Welsh. However, currently Welsh adults are assessed for dyslexia through the medium of English. This can create the kind of difficulties expressed in 'Student Voices' below.

Case Study: Sammi

Sammi's mother, like many, is concerned about her child; there is no specific cultural context.

Sammi's mother came to school with a friend to interpret for her because she wanted to tell the teacher that she was concerned about her son's reading. She could not read English herself, but she had seen other children make progress and thought that Sammi was not getting on as well as he could. She wondered whether this could be because she was ill while she was expecting him.

The teacher checked her records and found that Sammi's mother was indeed correct and that his reading skills were not developing as quickly as they might – this had been attributed to the fact that English was a second language for him. Sammi's teacher began work on a systematic, phonological programme in English with Sammi, hoping that this would help him. Sammi's teacher, mother and mother's friend all agreed to meet later in the school year in order to discuss his progress and plan the next steps.

Commentary: How might a Dyslexia-friendly teacher and school support Sammi?

It is important to reassure Sammi's mother and tell her that it is unlikely that her illness affected her son. It is important also to proceed with sensitivity bearing in mind any cultural background for Sammi's family. We may need to ask for continued translation support from a member of his mother's ethnic or cultural community, continuing with the practice of bringing a friend or community member to help in the discussion.

In order to gain more background information we might ask Sammi's mother whether she or any others in her family had any problems learning to read. Whether or not the answer is 'yes', we might say that we would like to assess her son to find out where his difficulty lies. We would have to explain what we mean by assessment, and we might ask, sensitively, whether his mother wishes Sammi to have a medical assessment in order to lay her fears at rest. If so, then the best route would be for the Sammi's mother to contact her GP and ask for a referral to a paediatrician.

It might not be advisable to mention dyslexia at this stage. It would be useful to know which language Sammi uses at home and whether he experiences any difficulties in other language contexts, such as when attending an ethnic community or religious school. We might explain that English is a very difficult language to learn because of the nature of the language. In eventually using the term 'dyslexia' we must take care to put it in the context of literacy difficulty, otherwise it may sound like an illness to Sammi's mother and link with her own fears about illness in pregnancy.

We need to provide further help for Sammi. A structured, multisensory, phonics programme could be put in place to give him an opportunity to understand the structure of written English. This might not be the first phonics intervention he has experienced, so we must take care to notice any confusion in Sammi's phonological understanding. We should also seek to develop his knowledge at the word, syllable and morpheme levels using Dyslexia-friendly approaches, and encourage opportunities for Sammi to demonstrate his strengths and interests in his school work.

Student Voices: Aled

Here are the words of Aled, a mature student who is also a parent. Aled is concerned about his daughter Bethan's literacy learning:

> *My daily life is lived in the Welsh language – I'm immersed in it. I hated school because of my lack of ability: there was no support network, no help, no support at home or in school, it was terrible. Spelling and punctuation were difficult in both Welsh and English. You could get away with it in Welsh because there are no hidden letters, and you pronounced it the way it is spelled; but in English there are silent 'k's and 'c's and so on. English was very hard for me – quite a downfall.*
>
> *I've been assessed for dyslexia in English. There are a few tests for dyslexia in Welsh and for children this is important, whereas for an adult being tested in English is OK. The problem is, I now see my daughter Bethan showing the same signs of dyslexia that I had, and still have. To test Bethan for dyslexia in English would be unfair, it would not show a true profile because English is hard, but to test Bethan in Welsh the questions would be easier, and again it would not show a true profile, so I don't know what to do for the best.* (Aled, an adult)

What might a Dyslexia-friendly teacher learn from this?

1. Aled is worried about his daughter – he needs to be reassured that her learning needs will be met in either language.
2. A Dyslexia-friendly teacher will notice that Aled thinks that his difficulties represent a lack of ability and will want to explain that this is not the case.
3. Aled may have discussed dyslexia with Bethan and she may be worried too. A knowledgeable, Dyslexia-friendly teacher would enable Aled to pass on useful information to Bethan.
4. Aled needs to be reassured that, unlike his school days, there is now a greater awareness of dyslexia and the need to support dyslexic learners. Aled is entitled to feel satisfied that Bethan's school is meeting her learning needs. He needs to discuss his concerns with the school and if he is not satisfied, he is entitled to pursue the matter.
5. The question of assessment is not one that can be easily resolved by a practitioner. Following discussion with Aled, his daughter's teacher needs to seek further advice about assessment from a specialist teacher or an educational psychologist.

Even if a school presently has no students who speak a different home language, that situation is not likely to continue for long, so schools need to take a multilingual stance as standard. To support the linguistic range the British Dyslexia Association website has a leaflet entitled *What Is Dyslexia* translated into 12 different languages, including Welsh, Chinese, Arabic and Urdu. This highlights the understanding that dyslexia is present in all nations but may be experienced and expressed differently according to the language spoken.

To navigate to this leaflet, on the BDA home page viewers need to open the tab 'About Dyslexia', then go to the menu on the left-hand side and click on 'Translated Dyslexia Information'. The resulting page is headed 'Dyslexia Information in Other Languages' and beneath this heading is a sentence including an underlined link, basic information. Clicking on this link opens the page 'What is Dyslexia' in English, while other languages are indicated by their flags on the previous web page.

Information and Communication Technology: Translation software

The development of mechanical language-to-language translation has been sought for some time, with an early application in translation into Braille. With the continuing increase in computing power, translation software has now become widely available as a free resource. Examples include Google Translate and Babylon 9 from Yahoo. There are also a number of commercial software programs, and Top Ten Reviews (see below for the website) offer a useful, graphically organised review of some of these.

The potential for teachers of using translation software in order to create dual-language resources is significant. It is well-known that translation software can make mistakes and practitioners will naturally want to check that usage is correct. It may also be necessary to print off and enlarge text in order to create resources; Google Translate does not offer a 'print' menu, but the text can be printed by pressing Ctrl+P. With a great range of languages, the accuracy and flexibility of translation software programs are sure to improve, providing a valuable resource for practitioners working in multilingual settings.

Homework: Parents scribing for their dyslexic child

Firman and Francica (2006), in discussing dyslexia in the dual language context of Malta, mention homework scribed by parents as an adjustment for students. Amid a useful list of suggestions regarding homework (via the 'About Dyslexia' page, 'Information for Parents' menu), the BDA website concurs:

> When necessary and appropriate, scribe for your child so that they can get their ideas on paper more accurately. (British Dyslexia Association, n.d.)

This raises the interesting question of how far parents can or should help their children with their homework. Scribing, that is writing down what they say, is a reasonable adjustment which is acceptable and even routine in classroom support and in some examinations. However, homework scribed at home raises issues of parental guilt for perhaps having done too much. Equally a student's work may be dismissed if it is thought to have been done by parents.

For a multilingual child who is possibly dyslexic, the scribing of homework may be a doubly-important strategy until s/he has gained necessary literacy skills. To avoid misunderstanding, this strategy can be agreed with a student's teachers. Parents may make a note in the margins of the homework to show that it is scribed and how long it took.

Revision: Putting short-term memory to work

Where learners with dyslexia are concerned, one key issue is memory, possibly more so than for other learners, since difficulties with short-term and working memory, and also procedural and declarative memory (Ullman, 2004), may be characteristic features. Declarative memory is concerned with the knowledge of memorised words, that is the lexicon; procedural memory is concerned with organisational, sequential and therefore grammatical processes. In dyslexia the question is always how to get knowledge about literacy and literacy-based information to be retained and/or retrieved, although multisensory methods increase the chances of memorisation.

Revision is often a preparation for examinations, and as a technique we can make use of short-term memory. If there is something that must be remembered, such as a date, a quote or three key points about a text, this can be revised right up to the time of entering the examination room, rehearsed mentally and then written down on rough paper before turning the examination paper and beginning the questions. A multilingual student may prefer to carry out this memorising in their home language. As a short-term memory technique this is necessarily restricted to a tiny packet of information; it will not take the place of a more widespread knowledge of the subject, but it could increase confidence for an examinee.

Five steps in moving to Dyslexia-friendly teaching for dyslexia and English as an additional language

Adopt a multilingual stance in policy and practice.

↓

Use Dyslexia-friendly methods to support language acquisition.

↓

If a child does not make expected progress in gaining English language, consider informal (and formal) dyslexia assessment.

↓

Consider realignment of conventional language programmes.

↓

Consider individual tuition using dyslexia specialist know-how.

Whole-school and whole-class strategies for dyslexia and English as an additional language

Table 4.1 considers school and class strategies that support language development for children for whom English is not the first language, and who may experience dyslexia. The table draws on a range of sources, notably Landon (2001), Schneider (2009) and Overington (2012).

Table 4.1 Whole-school and whole-class strategies for dyslexia and English as an additional language

	Early years	**Primary**	**Secondary**	**Tertiary**
Whole-school strategy	School takes multilingual stance, welcoming children and parents in a range of languages. Community cohesion is encouraged through cross-cultural activities.	School has clear and regular links with the EAL team. Bilingual TAs are recruited where possible. Policy shows understanding that not all English language delay is due to unfamiliarity.	School can demonstrate how it spends funds in supporting students with English as an alternative language and with dyslexia.	Policy reflects a consideration of dyslexia when a student does not make expected progress in English language acquisition.
	There is a system for liaising with community groups so that interpreters may be called upon if necessary. Staff pronounce unfamiliar names correctly, showing respect.	There is a system in place for liaising with the EAL team to identify readers and spellers who are falling behind and working with them. Further referral to assessment services is available.	There are dual-language resources and dyslexia support software available for students who have not made expected progress in English language acquisition. A system is in place for monitoring and evaluating progress, on a student level and on a school level.	A student who is still struggling with English at this stage is considered in terms of someone with severe dyslexia, and is provided with tuition and resources accordingly, in line with equality legislation and Codes of Conduct.
Whole-class strategy	Teaching encourages English speaking through play activities, multisensory activities, telling and re-telling of stories and parental involvement.	Teaching encourages the use of multisensory apparatus, games and activities, and also phonics input. These may need to continue for a longer time in supporting learning.	Teaching uses Dyslexia-friendly approaches in the teaching of English. Use of multisensory apparatus, games and activities and also phonics input continue if the student is willing.	Teaching includes discussion with learners about how best they learn, encouraging the development of metacognition.
	Literacy-based play and multisensory activities can continue for longer in support of English language learning.	Teachers consider dyslexia when a child is not making progress and can call on a range of informal assessments to identify possible dyslexia.	If difficulties continue, and if a referral has not previously been made, the advice of a practising psychologist should be sought.	Dyslexia support techniques for memory and sequencing are promoted alongside techniques for English language acquisition. Subject-specific vocabulary is taught.

Useful websites

- The National Association for Language Development in the Curriculum (NALDIC): http://www.naldic.org.uk
- Professional Association of Teachers of Students with Specific Learning Difficulties http://www.patoss-dyslexia.org/
- Top Ten Software Reviews:
  - for English Language learning: http://software.toptenreviews.com/foreign-languages/
  - for translation software: http://translation-software-review.toptenreviews.com

Further reading

Kelly, K. and Phillips, S. (2011) *Teaching Literacy to Learners with Dyslexia.* London: Sage.

Schneider, E. (2009) 'Dyslexia and foreign language learning', in G. Reid (ed.), *The Routledge Companion to Dyslexia.* Abingdon: Routledge.

Ziegler, J. and Goswami, U. (2005) 'Reading acquisition, developmental dyslexia, and skilled reading across languages: a psycholinguistic grain size theory', *Psychological Bulletin,* 131 (1): 3–29.

5

Reading, writing and spelling

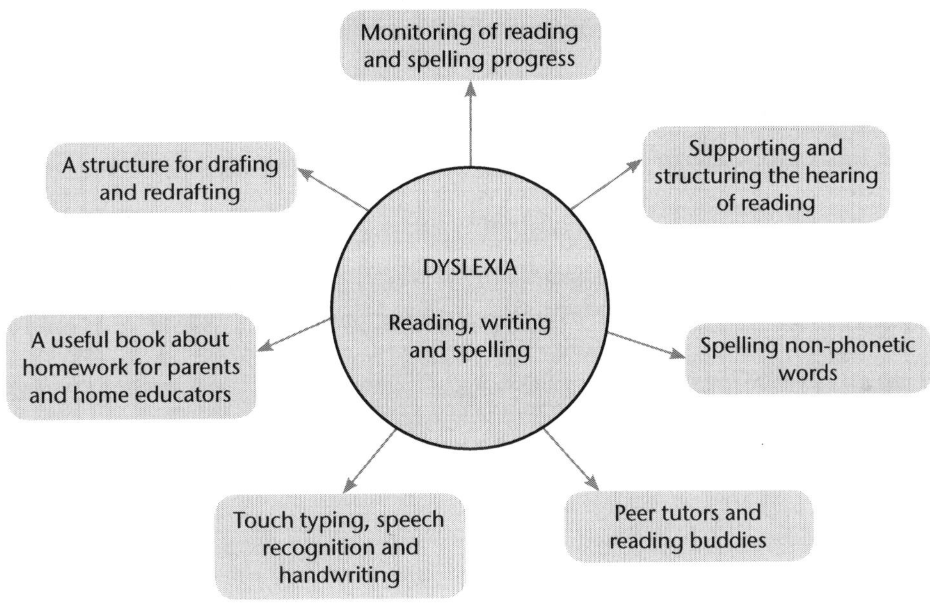

The use of structured phonics schemes has expanded from a dyslexia specialism to become mainstream practice. Dyslexia, while not completely understood, is less of a mystery, enabling practitioners to teach reading, writing and spelling with the knowledge that it can be overcome – but not made to disappear. It must not be forgotten that dyslexia occurs over a range, and some people will experience it more severely than others. For learners with this degree of difficulty, additional support and structured teaching will be needed over time.

Good Practice Points: Monitoring of reading or spelling progress

1. Maintaining a short, personalised, incremental reading or spelling record provides a helpful strategy to use with all students. The approach can also be used by parents, in liaison with the teacher. Use of an incremental checklist clarifies a student's own perception of what s/he is seeing or remembering.
2. Initially only a few words or sounds are given to practise, and once they are given they are not taken away when mastered. The list is increased with success, aiding positive reinforcement for a child who has difficulty. (Care must be taken that a short list is not seen negatively.) Constant practice improves speed of recollection.
3. If practised regularly, it becomes clear within a few weeks which students are finding learning sounds or sight words more difficult than their peers, so that the possibility of dyslexia can be monitored from this early stage. Signs that would make a Dyslexia-friendly teacher want to monitor more closely, might include intractable difficulties in:
   - confusing letters: b, d, p, q are often confused, as are m/w and u/n. In addition, it is common for vowels to be confused with each other;
   - visual confusion or disorientation: a student may be unsure in which direction to read a word causing *saw* to be read as *was*;
   - not being able to remember sounds and words previously mastered.
4. A teacher will understand the need to provide additional teaching if they find that the same sounds or words remain on the list for a length of time, unmastered. Such teaching will use multisensory methods, small steps and links to previous learning.
5. In order to become proficient readers and spellers, children with dyslexic tendencies will require significantly more opportunities than the majority of their peers for structured practice and focused teaching. Recording students' reading or spelling practice allows us to ensure that these opportunities are provided.

Figure 5.1 provides a photocopiable chart for use as a short, personalised, incremental record of a student's efforts to read target words.

Supporting and structuring the hearing of reading

Students may be given texts that are too hard for them to read in an effort to advance their skills. A useful tool for gauging the suitability of the material suggested by Peter Pumfrey (1985) is the Informal Reading Inventory (IRI). This counts the number of errors and can be used for any text or applied to a miscue analysis. Pumfrey suggests that the number of words in a passage may be reduced proportionately to match a struggling student's skill level. Such a passage may be based on 20, 40, 60, 80 or 100 words:

- *Independent Level* – The child reads fewer than 1 in 100 words incorrectly in any given passage. The material is perceived as 'Easy to read' and is well understood.
- *Instructional Level* – The child reads fewer than 5 words incorrectly in every 100. The material is perceived as presenting some difficulties but will be within their grasp.

Name	**Sheet number** (since the record began)

/ correct, ? no response, 'xyz' incorrect response, recording exactly what the student said.

After 6 correct responses in a row, celebrate! Then add a new word/sound to the list. Known words or sounds stay on the list in order to improve response time.

Word/ sound	**Date**															

Figure 5.1 A word/sound recognition monitoring sheet for reading and spelling

- *Frustration Level* – 12 in 100 words (i.e. 1 in 8) or *more* are read inaccurately. Any material which is so difficult that the student makes errors, is slow, hesitant, distractible or cannot readily understand the meaning is very frustrating for that reader. At this level of difficulty a child has little likelihood of improving either their skill in or attitude towards reading.

Hearing students read is an important part of helping them to gain literacy skills. The system of Pause, Prompt and Praise (Glynn et al., 2006) can help practitioners, mentors and family members hear students read by structuring the experience for them. The authors are specific about the prompts, using the reading record to provide a means of assessment that does not rely on normative procedures. They suggest that monitoring reading in this way helps teachers check on their own practice, as well as providing considerably detailed information about a learner's skills and approaches to reading.

In correspondence the authors stress the need for some practice in this process at first (Glynn, 2012). When tutors begin using Pause, Prompt and Praise, they benefit from having their timing checked, to make sure that they have waited the full five seconds before prompting. In addition they need to ensure that they give some priority to prompts about meaning, reinforcing the skills of reading within context. For practitioners who are in a work setting rather than training, supportive coaching of this kind can be done through peer-based, in-service tutoring.

Figure 5.2 is the recommended record form for Pause, Prompt, Praise (Glynn et al., 2006: 148). The form is completed left to right; the numbers 1–7 in the leftmost column refer to each word reading error. The authors suggest that this process can be completed from a tape recording as well as from live experience.

Reader		**Tutor response**								**Reader error correction**		
		PAUSE	**PROMPT**			**PRAISE**						
(1) Correct word from the text:	(2) Word read by mistake or word omitted	(3) Wait up to 5 seconds unless self-corrects before then	(4) To read on or read again	(5) To think about the meaning of the word	(6) To think about the look or sound of the word	(7) If reader word is nearly correct	(8) If reader self-corrects NO tutor help	(9) If reader uses a tutor prompt to correct error	(10) If reader tries hard or works well	(11) Reader self-corrects error without help from tutor	(12) Reader corrects error after tutor prompts	(13) Reader is told the word by tutor
1												
2												
3												
4												
5												
6												
7												

Figure 5.2 Glynn et al.'s (2006) monitoring form for Pause, Prompt, Praise

Wendy Spooner (2006) describes this process, noting the importance of ensuring that the level of readability is right. If a reader does not notice that they have made an error, their teacher/tutor stops them at the end of a phrase or a sentence and can encourage a student to look again. If there are too many such errors, this would suggest that the text is too difficult.

1. The child reads the passage to the teacher.
2. The child stops when he/she reaches an unknown word.
3. The teacher pauses to allow the child a short time to work out what the word is.
4. If the child is unable to work out what the word is, the teacher prompts the child, e.g. 'Can you guess what the word might be? Look at the initial letter – what sound does it make?' etc.
5. If the child produces the correct word the teacher praises him/her.
6. If the child does not produce the correct word or after the brief prompt, the teacher supplies the word.

The teacher also praises a student for self-correcting.

(Spooner, 2006: 38)

Spelling non-phonetic or 'tricky' words

Joshi and Carreker (2009) point out that spelling is not the same as reading. They separate the skill of reading, which is a matter of recognising words and where contextual cues can help, from the skill of recalling, which is required by spelling. Whichever phonics or reading scheme a school chooses, the delineation between reading and spelling is blurred initially; most students are able to spell simple, phonetically correct words before they are aware of the need to do so. They come to absorb rules or 'constraints' of spelling without direct instruction. However, Joshi and Carreker point out that

> Students with dyslexia usually do not intuit these constraints and need explicit attention to the constraints. (2009: 119)

When they are learning phoneme-to-grapheme skills, students practise breaking up words into their component parts, syllables or morphemes, and then breaking up the sounds within those elements, in a process known as 'segmenting'. While students may master regular phoneme-to-grapheme recoding, English has a number of confusing words which fall into the 'non-phonetic' category. They include key early words such as *the*, *was* and *people*. A useful example is '*choir*': How might choir be segmented?

c/h/o/i/r ?   ch/oi/r ?   ch/o/i/r ?

All are phonetically acceptable attempts, but none of them will result in the correct pronunciation.

One way to tackle this encourages students to recognise which part(s) of a 'tricky' word are the 'friendly' part(s) and which the tricky part, for reading or for spelling. Here the word 'was' is broken down:

w	a	s
Friendly. It says its sound	Tricky. It says the sound 'o'	Friendly. It says its sound

Taking this approach enables dyslexic learners to retain some sense of control over their spelling. It also encourages them to look carefully at the way a word is constructed, thus embedding it more fully in the visual and long-term memory. The colour of the text and/or background can link or separate parts of the word while the clay modelling technique (see Chapter 4) can support the memorisation of the 'tricky' element.

Something to Try: Students helping each other to learn in literacy

There are a number of arrangements where students help each other to gain literacy skills and the literature indicates that these can have positive outcomes. These include:

- peer-assisted learning where students take turns to guide and correct each other;
- peer-to-peer tutoring with students of about the same age, but with differing skill levels – a student with more highly developed literacy skills guides one who is less skilled;
- reading buddies, where an older student guides a younger, less-experienced one;
- volunteer reading involving younger students guided by older ones, or by volunteers who, with appropriate safeguarding measures, may include adults from the community.

This kind of student-interactive pedagogy can deepen learning and understanding for both students. Peer tutoring is especially powerful when used with older students (8+ years) who are falling behind. Some schools use peer tutoring very successfully, with 'reading buddies', working daily with younger students for a predetermined number of weeks. However, just bringing two students together will not suffice. As with any programme, careful monitoring of progress is vital.

Pointing out the opportunities for fun in this process, Tori Flint takes the view that:

> Students can learn as much and likely more while reading with a partner than while reading independently. (Flint, 2010: 296)

Conversely, Christ and Wang (2012) note that the process is undermined when buddies struggle over taking part, are confused about the reading roles or are confused about the content of their reading texts. This emphasises the importance of planning and goal setting, although, as the case study below shows, informal reading buddies can also help each other to good effect.

Case study: Jack and Jamie

Jack and Jamie were 5 years old and were best friends at school. Jamie had been very successful learning to read and write sounds from memory. His family owned a cafe near his home.

Jamie and Jack decided to play at 'cafes' one morning. Together they decided what to have on the menu. The teacher was aware of Jamie spelling out fish and chips, jelly (jely), chicken (chiken) and sandwiches (ham sanwich) on a whiteboard in the class. They discussed how to write 'coffee' – Jamie insisted that it was 'double ee and ff' as he could remember having seen it 'lots of times' in the cafe.

Their teacher observed them working in this way for almost an hour, making the menu and then taking turns to be the waiter writing down orders. As each new order was created the boys worked together decoding words into known phonemes. Not once did they worry that they were unable to spell a word. Their image of themselves was as competent writers.

Jack and Jamie were engaged in writing for far longer than their teacher expected because they were motivated to do so through their play. However, when their teacher looked at Jack and Jamie's order slips, there was a noticeable difference between them. Jack's writing was more uncertain, he used fewer words and the spelling was more rudimentary. Some words consisted only of a couple of beginning letters.

Commentary: How might a Dyslexia-friendly teacher and school support Jack?

A Dyslexia-friendly teacher will already have noticed the difference in literacy skills between Jack and Jamie. S/he will be monitoring Jack's progress in line with school policy, and considering interventions if it seems that he is not making progress at the preferred rate. The teacher may already have put some interventions in place and be monitoring their impact.

A responsive teacher will also be pleased to see the commitment that Jack is prepared to make to using written words, and will value the impact that Jamie's support is making, through his friendship and his more highly developed literacy skills. It is a two-way process because Jamie benefits from Jack's ideas, his involvement and his activities that facilitate the game, making it more vivid and more interesting.

Although this is not a constructed 'reading buddy' relationship, it is serving that purpose at this early stage. At some point, if Jack is not catching up, their teacher may ask Jamie to take a more regular 'buddy' role in helping Jack to make progress. A teacher choosing this route should talk to their parents about the benefits to both students, identifying it as a reciprocal process. Jamie will benefit from breadth and fluency as well as depth in his literacy experience.

Student Voices: Mari and Cameron

Here are the words of two older students, Mari and Cameron, each taking the role of 'reading buddy' to a younger student.

> *I really like helping Reece to do his sounds and read. I can see how much he's come on since we started. He reads much faster now.* (Mari aged 9, speaking of Reece aged 7)

> *I am proud of Jan. She can cut up really hard words now. Do you know Miss, she cut up 'elephant' today!* (Cameron aged 10 of Jan aged 5)

What might a Dyslexia-friendly teacher learn from this?

1. Both the younger and the older learners are fully engaged in the literacy activity and are finding it enjoyable.
2. A relaxed, informal, sociable approach can get results.
3. The younger ones are making progress and the older ones are consolidating knowledge.
4. There is a need to keep track of exactly what activities Mari and Cameron are undertaking with Reece and Jan.
5. There may be a need to coach Mari and Cameron carefully in their work with Reece and Jan, especially if their younger buddy's difficulties are intractable and possibly dyslexic in nature.

Information and Communication Technology: Touch-typing, speech recognition and handwriting

Access to ICT is a recognised asset for students who experience dyslexia, from primary school upwards. Students who are slower in expressing themselves through handwriting will also be slow expressing themselves through word-processing. Researchers found a strong correlation between handwriting speed and typing speed, and the handwritten form was consistently faster (Connolly et al., 2007).

Dyslexic students will not be especially advantaged in word-processing prose unless they also receive fairly substantial systematic training in touch-typing, also known as automatic keyboarding. Students who are able to have input of this kind (over about 8 weeks) are able to improve the length and quality of the essays they write on the keyboard (Connolly et al., 2007, citing Christensen, 2004).

Another way of producing written work is through speech recognition. Speech recognition programs for word-processing have to be trained in advance by the speaker. Speech recognition software often comes ready-installed within a computer's Ease of Access settings and is improving with each generation of computers. It may be helpful to dictate with eyes shut, and then read and correct the text afterwards.

Alternatively, there is a view that writing words by hand brings about improved understanding of reading and that writing letters in script integrates perception and motor skills. It seems likely that dyslexic students can benefit from all three forms of writing practice, but in order to be able to make full use of the potential for word-processing of their written work, they need to learn to touch-type.

A free touch-typing program from the BBC, used with headphones is *Dance Mat Typing*. *Nessy Fingers* (Net Education Ltd) teaches keyboard skills and spelling at the same time. DyslexiaAction offers touch-typing tuition, and offers the touch typing program *Englishtype* in junior and senior versions (Englishtype Ltd).

Homework: A useful book for parents and home educators

Dyslexia is fatiguing, and after a long school day dyslexic students do not find it easy to continue with tasks that they have already found difficult and dispiriting. To address this difficulty Neil MacKay, the originator of the Dyslexia-friendly concept, has a helpful book for parents and home educators, called *Taking the Hell out of Homework*. This is a small, illustrated book which transfers Dyslexia-friendly teaching and learning strategies out of the classroom and into a home setting, both for general learning and for literacy. Of particular interest for reading, writing and spelling is MacKay's Make And Break technique (pp. 58/9), where words are segmented, stretched, recombined and visualised. The book is available from SEN Books Ltd.

Revision: A structure for drafting and redrafting

Teaching expects the revision and redrafting of written work at all levels, but key assumptions about this are confounded by the experience of dyslexia. For example, a step-by-step sequence that seems logical to a teacher or a parent may not be obvious at all to a dyslexic student. Memory difficulties may make it hard to sustain and develop an argument, and a sentence that is too long may end on a different topic from the one where it started. Being corrected, or told to correct, for errors will not help a dyslexic student; they may not be able to spot the errors in the first place, and if errors are successfully identified, they may not be able to tell what is the correct word and why. Even if these difficulties are successfully negotiated, there is the matter of correctness of spelling, and also the tendency to use a safe vocabulary instead of a more sophisticated but risky one that reveals a deeper level of knowledge.

All these considerations challenge teachers' assumptions of how to help students improve their work by drafting. The writing of some dyslexic students will seem chaotic because of difficulties in the conventional structuring and shaping of a piece of work. Nor is it helpful to tell students in detail how to structure their work; this will lead to overload and confusion.

Some dyslexic learners find the Outline function in Microsoft Word to be helpful; it is found in the View menu of Word (Windows 7). This allows points to be lined up under headings and sub-headings, and then when the view is changed, they become normal text. The 'trick' is to remember to use the arrows at either side of the Levels window in Outline in order to insert headings and subheadings. Organising a piece of writing through this process can promote greater clarity.

For many pieces of writing, a simple 'background-present position-way forward' formula will provide a useful structure, perhaps 'topped' with an introduction and 'tailed' with a conclusion. Combining BG-PP-WF with Outline gives an instant structure into which the student can then distribute the points they want to make, either as a first draft, or as a way of sorting points already made. There are other methods and styles of writing, but for organising a draft or re-draft to create a logical order, this will work.

Five steps in moving to Dyslexia-friendly approaches for reading, writing and spelling

Have a school-wide, phonics-based reading and spelling strategy followed by all members of staff, including ancillary staff.

↓

Keep consistent, careful records to monitor rates of progress.

↓

Identify slower rate of progress at an early stage.

↓

Ensure that identification leads to teaching intervention.

↓

Train reading buddies in Dyslexia-friendly approaches to reading and spelling.

Whole-school and whole-class strategies for reading, writing and spelling

Table 5.1 considers school and class strategies that support the development of literacy skills across the range of educational phases and stages.

Table 5.1 Whole-school and whole-class strategies for reading, writing and spelling

	Early years	**Primary**	**Secondary**	**Tertiary**
Whole-school strategy	School includes an optional question on enrolment information forms asking parents whether they would like to discuss dyslexia or any other learning characteristic for their child. If 'yes', there is a system for following up carefully and informing class teachers and SENCO, with parents' permission.	School promotes use of a class 'Wow! word wall' to collate interesting, new, powerful words which are referred to regularly and changed often. School has a policy of giving only short spelling tests. Spelling tests include some familiar and some unfamiliar words.	School expects all teachers to be clear about the objectives of each lesson and provides staff training and opportunities for discussion to this end[1]. Schools accept the need to allow possible or diagnosed dyselxic learners to use their own strategies for successful learning, such as use of ICT to record or write notes, and use of a laptop computer for written work.	Strategy is to provide Dyslexia-friendly pedagogical training for mainstream practitioners. This includes accepting the use of students' recording devices in lectures and accepting that students may need to photograph a diagram or display. Practitioner training emphasises that not all students can read rapidly. Pedagogical practice does not require students to watch slide presentations, listen to lecturers, read handouts and take notes, all at the same time.
Whole-class strategy	Children see adults writing with reason every day. Adults explain what they are doing as they 'write with reason'. Children are told the same story, or read the same book, for a week, giving them opportunities to learn story sequence and vocabulary, and to develop an understanding that print carries meaning.	Children are introduced to various methods to learn spellings for tests. Visual – look, say, write, check. Auditory – look, say, check, repeat. Kinaesthetic – write with finger in the air, on parent's back, in flour on work surface, with felt tips on paper, saying each letter as doing so.	Teachers write legibly on whiteboards, particularly when introducing new or key vocabulary. They write a maximum of five lines. In subjects where there is a lot of new vocabulary to learn at a time, a list of written key vocabulary is given to students. New vocabulary is repeated often in a lesson and used in context.	Practitioners provide subject-specific key terms and phrases, and glossaries for all, particularly in support of students who find reading long new words difficult or who have trouble remembering them. Practitioners keep teacher talk to a minimum. They provide short, simple explanations of words or concepts as a matter of course.

[1]Literacy targets are included.

Useful websites

- Advice for parents: http://www.mumsnet.com/books/teach-your-child-to-read/
- For phonic, letter formation and spelling practice on i-Phone or i-Pad: http://www.appsinmypocket.com/
- For the touch-typing programmes mentioned above:
  - http://www.bbc.co.uk
  - http://www.nessyfingers.co.uk
  - http://www.englishtype.com

Further reading

Department for Children, Schools and Families (2009) *Support for Spelling* (2nd edn). Nottingham: DCSF.

Joshi, R. M. and Carreker, S. (2009) 'Spelling: development, assessment and instruction', in G. Reid (ed.), *The Routledge Companion to Dyslexia*. Abingdon: Routledge.

MacKay, N. (2010) *Taking the Hell Out of Homework*. Wakefield: SEN Marketing. Available at: http://www.senbooks.co.uk.

6

Dyslexia and mathematics

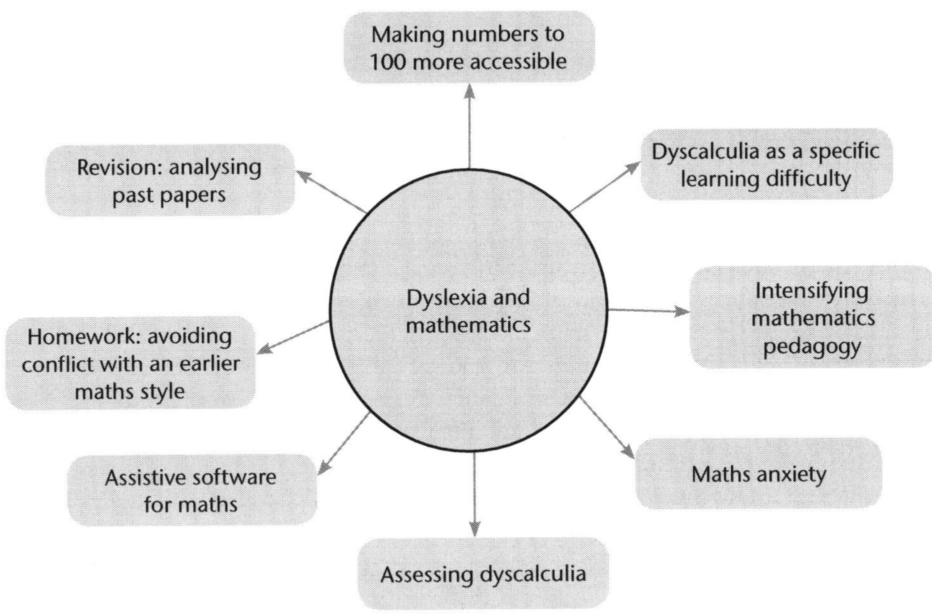

There has been much debate about dyslexia and mathematics, since not all students with dyslexia have problems with mathematics. If a persistent difficulty with numeracy and/or mathematics is a separate specific learning difficulty (SpLD) called dyscalculia, individuals with dyslexia who experience mathematical difficulties could be said to have the co-occurring difficulties of dyscalculia and dyslexia. In any event, a difficulty with mathematics has to be addressed so that students can reach their full potential. Some students with dyslexia will have definite problems with mathematics, and just as with the uniqueness of students' experience of dyslexia, mathematics difficulties will also be expressed in a unique way. Even if a student does not experience dyscalculia, someone who finds reading difficult will almost certainly find reading and perhaps interpreting mathematical text problematic. A difficulty in mathematics can have as much of an impact as a reading difficulty.

Good Practice Points: Making numbers to 100 more accessible

1. From the start, young students should be encouraged to learn and hear numbers beyond 10. This is especially true for children who may manifest dyslexic traits.
2. Most classrooms contain at least one 100 square. Experience suggests that a 0–99 square is easier for dyslexic students to use as the 'tens barriers' are at the start of the line rather than at the end. This makes it easier for children to track along lines and locate numbers. A reproducible example of a 0–99 table square can be found at the Innovative Classroom website (see chapter end for the web address).
3. At some stage students need to learn the multiplication tables. If these are to be learned by memory, as a class activity, then having a visual prompt is valuable to dyslexic and non-dyslexic learners alike.
4. We advocate a return to old-style multiplication tables posters displayed on the wall, with one poster per multiplication table, well-presented.
5. As multiplication tables carry a lot of information which is usually presented close together, these need to be written in a large, clear font or in skilled handwriting using a broad felt-tip pen.
6. Posters might be taken down temporarily for a test of multiplication tables. But:
7. Modern understanding will differentiate such tests in the same way that spelling tests might be differentiated, with only a few targets at a time.
8. For older students flexible table squares can be excellent 'ready reckoners'. These are relatively small, plastic sheets containing multiplication tables, the sheets being folded to highlight various rows and columns.
9. There are tables for multiplication, addition, percentages and fractions available from the Flexitable website (web address at the end of the chapter).
10. There is debate about what kind of font (for numbers and for letters) is best for dyslexic learners. The British Dyslexia Association concludes that it is rather the case that the best font is the one that an individual student prefers.
11. When it comes to numbers it is advisable to choose a sans serif font, that is a font without a serif or 'hook' to the numeral one (1, as in this example); this avoids possible confusion with the numeral 7.
12. Some fonts contain a curled 9 which is easy for dyslexic students to confuse with a 6; similarly some 2 numerals look too similar to a reversed 5.
13. A crucial building block for every student is the understanding of the number names and the numbers which they represent. It is unfortunate that every number up to 20 is different and must be learned as an individual entity.
14. The names for the 'teen' numbers do not follow the same rule as numbers past 20 – if they did 'sixteen' would rightly be called 'teensix'!
15. Students may understand the pattern of numbers past 20 more easily because they can follow the pattern of the '*tens* number name first followed by the *units* number name'.
16. Sometimes students with dyslexia or dyscalculia will take an answer from a previous question and relocate it to the next page or to the top of the same page. The term 'perseveration' is used to describe this process, and teachers should look out for apparent perseveration errors, since they are not, of themselves, erroneous.
17. In marking work using numbers or words, it is now accepted as good practice to mark the steps in the process rather than ultimate answers, and to mark as correct the positives rather than mark critically, focusing on correcting errors.

18. In the marking process Dyslexia-friendly practice advocates avoiding the use of red ink as this has negative connotations for many students – confidence is undermined by years of such marking. We would suggest using green ink, but some students prefer the colour red, so this is an area where a supportive teacher might ask students about their preferences and a school may include this possibility in their marking policy.

There may be an analogy between numeracy or number sense with regard to mathematics and phonemic development with regard to reading (Gersten and Chard, 2001). *Numeracy*, a fluid and proficient use of numbers, is the prerequisite for mathematics, just as phonological development is for reading, although numeracy is less dependent on auditory processing (Smedt and Boets, 2010). Unlike reading, a taught skill, there is evidence that a sense of number is innate. The term for this is *numerosity*, which refers to the innate ability to judge the number of objects in a small set, either as an approximate number or as the exact number. According to Butterworth (2010) a deficit in this inherited ability is the cause of dyscalculia.

Dyscalculia as a specific learning difficulty

An exact definition of dyscalculia has not been agreed, but a persistent difficulty in acquiring arithmetical skills, together with a lack of number sense, is experienced by individuals with this learning profile. Misreading numbers or symbols (× instead of +) and transposing numbers (reading 57 for 75) are common difficulties. Trouble with interpreting symbols will affect the procedures selected to solve an arithmetical problem.

The Department for Education and Skills Numeracy Strategy definition states:

> Dyscalculia is a condition that affects the ability to acquire mathematical skills. Dyscalculic learners may have a difficulty understanding simple number concepts, lack an intuitive grasp of numbers, and have problems learning number facts and procedures. Even if they produce a correct answer or use a correct method, they may do so mechanically and without confidence. (DfES 2004)

Something to Try: Intensifying mathematics pedagogy for dyslexic students

Pre-school children learn mathematics from the language and logic that adults around them use and so a child may come into school with some knowledge of number and be quite confident. If a student does not have a good sense of number this must be taught.

1. *Apparatus*. Dyslexic and dyscalculic students may need to use three-dimensional apparatus for longer, and this must be made available in a way that does not embarrass older students. Examples of resources that can be used to make problems 'concrete' include Cuisenaire rods, Stern blocks and Numicon (Oxford University Press, n.d.). All these will help in multisensory teaching, which is vitally important for individuals who learn by doing.

2. *Visualisation.* It is helpful to visualise numbers in order to help reinforce addition to 10. For example, a child may think that a 2 is like a swan and an 8 is like a snowman – and the image of a swan and a snowman holding hands may make the number 10 come to mind more readily than saying the words for a student who is not retaining the number bond by conventional means. (This is only appropriate where students have a good visual memory and can use their own images.)
3. *Cooperative/collaborative learning.* When students work in pairs and/or groups, they can learn different ways to view a problem from their peers. If the atmosphere in the group is positive, this can help to build up the confidence of students with mathematics difficulties and develop their conceptual thinking.
4. *Estimating and checking.* Encouraging students to estimate the answer for a mathematics question will help them to know when to check their result if it is different. Using a different method to check the result increases accuracy. For example, for addition a student may add numbers from the top down and check the answer by adding the numbers from the bottom up.
5. *Remembering the 'teen' numbers.* Some dyslexic and dyscalculic children will fully understand and remember the 'teen' numbers so that they can go on to learn tens and units. If children are not ready for this, attention can be drawn to the differently patterned, 'non-conformist' numbers by calling them 'three-teen/thirteen, four-teen/fourteen, five-teen/ fifteen'. This juxtaposition of the spoken names can jog a student's memory. Alternatively, we can try saying 'teen-four/fourteen' to highlight the numbering pattern which holds true once numbers over 20 are reached.

Maths anxiety

Some students develop anxiety and fear when they work with numbers. In extreme circumstances this can be expressed in the same way as any anxiety, with sweaty palms, heart palpitations, breathlessness and nausea. This anxiety does not diminish unless the student finds a teacher who can explain maths in an appropriate way or the student manages to work through the difficulty. This negative, affective response to mathematics has a direct effect on students' ability to perform in mathematics tests (Rubinstein and Tannock, 2010). Teachers may experience maths anxiety themselves, and they need to be aware of this so as not to transfer this anxiety to students (Bekdemir, 2010).

As students with dyslexia can be prone to stress which in turn exacerbates their dyslexia, a student with dyslexia and/or dyscalculia/maths anxiety may suffer more from stress in maths sessions and be less able to fulfil their potential unless they have their stress levels taken into account and are given the necessary support. For a student who is performing poorly in mathematics, the first consideration might be whether they are experiencing mathematics anxiety.

An understanding of how this can interfere with learning leads a teacher to realise that no amount of reiterated explanation will help; it only increases the anxiety. Similarly, punishing or disciplining students will not aid them to acquire this learning. It is necessary to break down the mathematical learning into very small steps, until a point is found where the student truly understands, and then a teacher can reinforce this with praise and celebration. As with dyslexia, it may be that the learning is not retained or retrieved easily and needs to be revisited more than once.

The Williams Report (2008) reviewed mathematics teaching in the Early Years and found that mathematics success depends on having a qualified teacher with secure mathematics. One-to-one support was the most beneficial intervention along with some group work. Overlap of material in the one-to-one session with the daily mathematics lesson also reinforced learning and allowed students to build up their confidence. However, differentiation of teaching may perhaps be even better. Engaging the help of parents in working with the student was also found to be important.

Case Study: Sonja

Sonja was always the last to put up her hand whenever the teacher asked questions in maths lessons. If ever the teacher asked her to answer Sonja's answer was always the same 'Oh, I forget now'. Little by little Sonja lost interest and confidence in her maths ability.

Her teacher talked with Sonja, and Sonja admitted that sometimes she put her hand up when she had no answer just so her class mates thought she was keeping up with everyone else. Sonja said sometimes she could think of the answer but by the time she had worked it out the teacher had moved on.

Now Sonja's teacher asks Sonja her own specific targeted questions. Her classmates understand that only Sonja can answer these questions and that she may need a little longer to think of the answer. Little by little Sonja's confidence is returning.

Commentary: How might a Dyslexia-friendly teacher and school support Sonja?

A Dyslexia-friendly teacher and school would expect to support Sonja's confidence in her learning, as well as supporting the new learning itself, and to use appropriate methods for doing so. These would include multisensory teaching, small steps in learning, alternative methods of recording and finding a way to enable Sonja to see the bigger picture of where the learning is headed, without undermining her confidence further.

A clear idea of what needs to be learned, step by step, helps both teacher and learner. When, in spite of best efforts, a student is not gaining a mathematical concept, a teacher may use the process of task analysis and 'backward chaining' to support teaching and learning. This can be used in any context. A teacher works backwards from the concept that they want a student to gain, asking themselves – 'what does my student need to know how to do in order to arrive at this point?' In this way the logical progression of steps is revealed which is needed to advance understanding to the point of acquiring the concept.

Working backwards through small steps in this way ultimately brings a teacher to the point where they find a student's secure understanding. Having found that starting point of secure knowledge, teaching can go forward in small stages, putting in place the building blocks to reach the end-point of the desired mathematical concept. A student's confidence must be supported when introducing the new learning, and this can be helped by using recognised dyslexia-friendly pedagogy. This learning may sometimes take place out of the main classroom, in the same way that a dyslexic student may need help with literacy outside of the classroom setting.

Assessing dyscalculia

While dyscalculia is presently a contested concept, much work is being done to explore it. Butterworth et al. (2011) suggest that dyscalculia has a basis in a difference in brain activity which corroborates Landerl et al.'s (2009) conclusion that a difficulty in arithmetic is independent of a difficulty in reading at a neurocognitive level. Accordingly, in Butterworth's Dyscalculia Screener (2003) for 6–14 years, numerosity in the form of dot enumeration is tested along with number comparison, reaction time and arithmetic achievement. Emmerson and Babtie's (2010) assessment tool allows teachers to ascertain a student's areas of difficulty and design an individual learning plan to help them to make progress.

A post-16 assessment of individual learning needs in the UK involves an initial screen for dyscalculia, a full assessment of verbal and non-verbal cognitive abilities, a standardised test of mathematical ability compared with age expectation, and a full personal history, particularly with regard to mathematics, as well as observed test behaviour for indications of mathematical anxiety or tension and lack of confidence in tackling mathematical calculations and problems. A post-16 screener, DyscalculiUM, has been developed by Trott and Beacham (2006) which also tests for number sense as well as number comparison, graph-reading, multiplication tables, time and symbolic abstraction, among other skills.

Student Voices: Millie and Declan

Here are the voices of Millie and Declan, both of whom are primary school students:

> *I thought I couldn't do maths. I always got my sums wrong when I thought I'd done them right. When I got in Mr Miller's class he asked me what I did with my sums, so I told him. Mr Miller saw I'd got it right but I'd read it the wrong way. Now he does me dots so I know where to start. I can do maths now.* (Millie aged 6 ¾)

> *The first time I counted all the way up to one hundred properly I ran downstairs to tell my mum. She wrote a note to tell Miss Bell. I got two merits for it.* (Declan aged 7)

What might a Dyslexia-friendly teacher learn from this?

It is important that, where a student is having difficulties, teachers talk to their student.

1. When a teacher understands the process that a student has gone through it may become apparent that they have some arithmetic skills in place. For example, they could understand the process of addition and subtraction but perhaps be reading the numbers from right to left.
2. Other dyslexic/dyscalculic types of errors to watch for could include: confusing the numbers (2 and 5, 6 and 9, 3 and 8, 1 and 7), and putting the right number in the wrong place.
3. If the sum is calculated as the child has done, we may be able to see that they are succeeding more than was thought.
4. It is important to protect a student's confidence in the face of mathematical difficulty. When mathematics concepts are demystified, and perhaps related to common sense and everyday experience, this can help.

Information and Communication Technology: Assistive software for mathematics

Teachers need to feel competent about ICT in order for students to make the most of the software available. It is possible that students may find individual i-Pads more accessible than computers since they allow students to pursue their own learning. They can allow students to work at their own pace and use visual formats of questions to help develop concepts.

Assistive software can help students overcome some of their mathematics difficulties. For example, text-to-speech software may help a student who has a difficulty with reading maths problems. A variety of software is available for drawing graphs and diagrams, and using statistics. MathTalk™ (Multiplex Voice Computing Inc. 2012) and Dragon Naturally Speaking (Nuance Communications Inc. 2012) allow the pupil to dictate maths text. There are specialised spellcheckers for spelling maths terms, and the use of an online thesaurus can help a student define terms.

When dyslexic students use calculators it is important that they have their eyes directly over the display when entering or reading digits. A two-line display scientific calculator may help a student to keep a mathematics problem in mind when working through it. When using calculators in examinations, students should be given a few minutes extra to familiarise themselves with different equipment.

Homework: Avoiding conflict with an earlier mathematics style

Maths homework in primary school needs careful thought. Maths teaching has changed considerably in the UK since the introduction of the Numeracy Strategy which gave UK teachers a national method for teaching methods of computation. The methods taught to children are not always the same as parents use. When parents or grandparents try to help by using the older methods that they learned themselves, it may be possible to create more confusion for a child who is already struggling. To avoid this possibility, more appropriate homework tasks may be set, such as maths games, or shape, space, measurement or data collection tasks.

At secondary and higher levels homework tends to consist of sets of exercises which have to be worked through. It is important that a student knows not to spend too much time on a problem if they cannot work through it. It may be better for dyslexic students to put that problem aside for half an hour, or until another evening, if possible. This allows a student to relax and come back to the problem afresh. Sometimes a student may be too tired to think and may need a good night's sleep before s/he can focus on the problem productively.

Revision: Analysing past papers

Revision implies that the student is returning to a subject already understood. Certain definitions or formulae may have to be learned but generally students need to practise problem-solving and mathematical procedures in preparation for examinations. If a mathematical procedure is difficult to remember although understanding has been achieved, then mnemonics or a visual memory link can help a student to connect up the logical progression and gain automaticity.

Phase	**Action**	**Timescale**
Phase 1: Organisation	Consider past papers. ↓ Note the total number of topics covered in all papers. ↓ Cluster questions and parts of questions on each topic. ↓ List topics to appear on the next paper and number them with the most likely topic first.	7 weeks before the exam
Phase 2: Explore your current knowledge	Attempt all questions 'cold' in the most likely topic. If you cannot solve a problem, let it go and move on to the next question. ↓ Do the same for all topics. ↓ Note the topics in which you feel secure.	6 weeks before the exam
Phase 3: Find the gaps	1. Take each topic in order and list what you need to look up, for example definitions, formulae or procedures. 2. Plug the gaps in your knowledge by making flashcards or verbally recording your answers.	5 weeks before the exam
Phase 4: Rehearse and reinforce	1. Rehearse the examination questions by testing your knowledge. 2. Attempt the questions under exam conditions until you can work through them satisfactorily.	4 weeks before the exam and up to the exam

Figure 6.1 A revision technique for mathematics: analysing past papers

Solving many different questions in the area being examined is the way to gain understanding and confidence, and this is true at all levels from the most basic to the postgraduate level at university. It is important not to get bored when revising and the Internet can provide a variety of websites. Recordings of lectures on aspects of maths are available on most topics, including further and higher education levels of mathematics.

Working through past papers for public examinations is extremely helpful, especially if the candidate monitors the time spent on the test. Figure 6.1 provides a schedule for analysing past mathematics papers in preparation for a maths examination.

Five steps in moving to Dyslexia-friendly mathematics practice

Be aware of possible maths difficulty experienced by students with dyslexia.

↓

Make sure that students with maths difficulties have any difficulties well-assessed, using valid, up-to-date assessment materials.

↓

Provide individual and group work to support students with maths difficulties.

↓

Help parents to understand their child's difficulties and involve them in intervention, using agreed computation methods.

↓

Support the provision of short-term teaching interventions across the school.

Whole-school and whole-class strategies for a mathematics focus

Table 6.1 considers school and class strategies that support mathematics development in relation to dyslexia.

Table 6.1 Whole-school and whole-class strategies for a mathematics focus

	Early years	**Primary**	**Secondary**	**Tertiary**
Whole-school strategy	The importance of mathematics is reflected in policy and practice. Staff are made aware of maths anxiety.	School policy for mathematics teaching reflects Dyslexia-friendly methods. Knowledge of dyscalculia is disseminated.	The subject-focused curriculum allows students to use preferred methods in problem-solving wherever possible. Mathematics ICT is available to all students.	Strategy reflects possible late identification of dyslexia or dyscalculia and makes arrangements and adjustments accordingly.
	There is a process to evaluate students' ability in mathematics. A wide range of apparatus is explored to exploit multisensory teaching to the full.	There is a system in place for noticing and identifying students who have difficulty with mathematics. An assessment for dyscalculia is available.	Where a student is having difficulties, particularly with arithmetic or symbol confusion, but not concepts, there is assessment for dyslexia and appropriate teaching is put in place.	All staff understand that dyslexic students may not be able to do mental arithmetic but may still be able to understand higher mathematical concepts.
Whole-class strategy	Teaching encourages an attitude of maths as fun, so that all students have equal opportunity to use their mathematical abilities.	Teachers are aware that the language of mathematics can be ambivalent and confuse dyslexic students.	Teachers recognise that students with SpLDs can excel in some mathematics topics, e.g. geometry, but not others, e.g. algebra.	Teachers recognise that number reversal and symbol confusion may indicate dyslexia which is not related to IQ.
	Teacher uses multisensory techniques, e.g. the use of songs and rhymes, to make maths memorable and enjoyable.	Working in pairs or groups is encouraged so students can learn different strategies from each other.	Minor mathematical errors are not focused on but strategies are devised to minimise their occurrence.	Multisensory teaching is still a feature of the pedagogy.

Useful websites

- About Dyscalculia: http://www.aboutdyscalculia.org/index.html
- Dynamo Maths: http://www.dynamomaths.co.uk
- For 0–99 number square: http://www.innovativeclassroom.com/
- For flexible multiplication and calculation squares: http://www.flexitable.co.uk/

Further reading

Bird, R. (2007) *The Dyscalculia Toolkit*. London: Sage.

Emmerson, J. and Babtie, P. (2010) *The Dyscalculia Assessment*. London: Continuum.

Hannell, G. (2005) *Dyscalculia: Action Plans for Successful Learning in Mathematics*. London: David Fulton.

7

Dyslexia and science

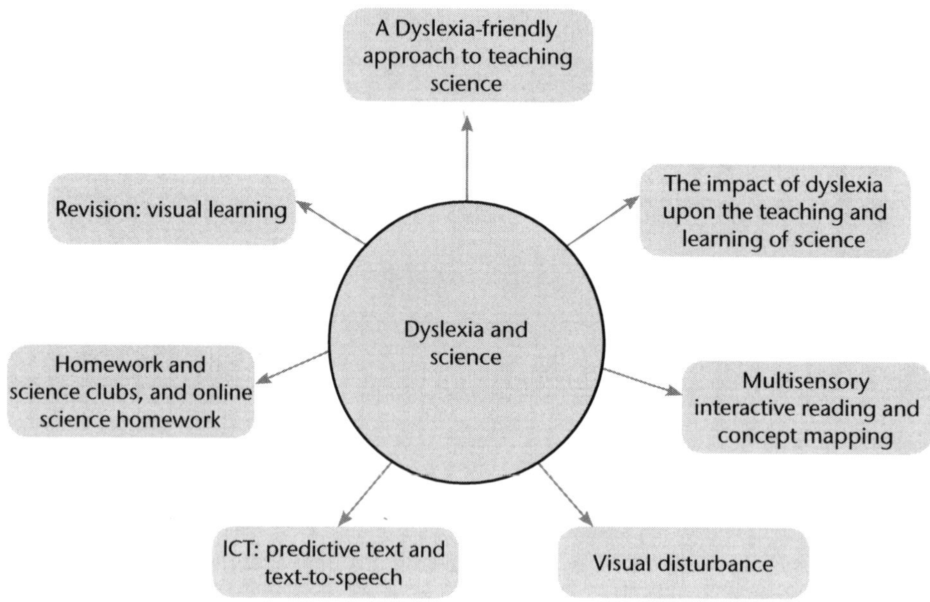

We are naturally curious about the world around us and the exploration of the environment is a good starting point from which to channel children's natural curiosity, imagination and enthusiasm. Observation and analysis are key skills in the development of science which is based on theories about the way the natural world operates. Constructing models of nature is necessary to understand the balance of the earth's resources and manage them responsibly and sustainably. Science is fundamental to developing thinking and is an important area of human endeavour, but it is by setting science in the context of human living that the socio-economic value of science can be demonstrated in concrete terms.

Good Practice Points: A Dyslexia-friendly approach to teaching science

All science teaching relies to a lesser or greater degree on mathematics, so all the advice given in Chapter 6 concerning teaching dyslexic students applies also to science. As in the acquisition of mathematics, gaining scientific knowledge relies heavily, although not exclusively, on stepwise learning. The first steps have to be understood and consolidated in order to make progress to the next level of understanding. Dyslexic students may require additional input in order to secure the steps. The following points show how input may be intensified:

1. Science teaching has to be multisensory to facilitate teaching and learning. Enabling dyslexic students to understand and achieve in this way means that the field of study may benefit more fully from the contributions of talented dyslexic students.

2. Multisensory teaching methods and diagrams include the use of flow charts and mindmaps. These can be used to give specific attention to scientific terms by writing them on the board and giving their etymology.

3. Students working together, in pairs or groups, have been shown to encourage enthusiasm in science learning.

4. A workbook for learning topics is better than single-sheet handouts or making students copy from the board, because notes are better organised and kept in one place, particularly when recording experiments. A bound laboratory book is essential in tertiary education.

5. Providing a scaffold for scientific writing, for example an outline showing how to write up an experiment, can help as an intermediate stage in developing formal scientific writing (see Figure 7.1 later in the chapter).

6. Students who find it difficult to listen and write notes at the same time, can focus on understanding the work if handouts are provided for them in advance so that they may annotate them.

7. Dyslexic students who are better visual learners and respond well to visual materials may still need time to interpret or process graphs and charts and write down their analysis.

8. Students with dyslexia benefit from repetition and reinforcement, so it is helpful to give an overview of the experiment at the beginning of a practical session.

9. Enough time needs to be provided for learning practical techniques until they become automatic.

10. It is important to check a student's work often and to establish links between findings and the original topic or research question in order to facilitate a student's enquiry.

A teacher's enthusiasm for science is infectious and needs to be sustained because it can inspire students. Enthusiasm and enjoyment in the study of science leads to achievement and success in learning and a positive attitude. All of these good qualities encourage dyslexic students to gain resilience to overcome their difficulties.

The impact of dyslexia upon the teaching and learning of science

Science is a practical subject; it requires a specific approach whereby a question or hypothesis is postulated and a method devised to put this question to the test. As science is primarily content driven and is largely mathematical, particularly in the case of the physical sciences, e.g. physics and chemistry, individuals who are less adept at languages but have an aptitude for understanding mathematics can succeed more readily in this area. Many dyslexic students fall into this category and indeed some famous scientists, for example Thomas Edison and Michael Faraday, are obvious examples. A recent small study in one university showed that twice as many dyslexic students in HE took science degrees as took arts degrees (Meehan, 2008).

Scientific textbooks are usually dense with facts and scientific jargon, so students with dyslexia may have problems keeping up with course reading. Frequently texts have to be reread to gain comprehension because so much energy is involved in decoding the words that meaning is lost. If students have attention difficulties they may reach the end of a page or section and have no recollection of what they have read because they lost focus.

Reading aloud may be particularly difficult, so giving a presentation may also prove difficult because pronouncing words, reading symbols, reading at speed and reading tables, all of which may be necessary, can be problematic. Although students with dyslexia may study science because there is less essay writing, accuracy in the use of language is necessary. It can be physically exhausting for students to write down their thoughts in a linear fashion. Interconnected thoughts enter their minds more rapidly than their speed of writing and trying to hold on to these, sort them out and put them into logical order can be an arduous task.

Spelling technical words may be difficult as words may differ only slightly, for example encephalitis (inflammation of the brain by a virus) and encephalomyelitis (inflammation of the brain and spinal cord), yet they have to be accurate. Listening and writing simultaneously is a difficult task for students with dyslexia and therefore note-taking can be difficult or impossible.

Organising complex tasks or performing a number of simple tasks simultaneously can be extremely difficult for a dyslexic student, but is necessary in a practical session when an experiment has to be finished within a definite time frame. Examples of common difficulties in organising student life include filing course notes and meeting deadlines for submitting work. Remembering days, dates and times of events is often difficult. Stress has the effect of increasing dyslexic traits and, in certain circumstances, may result in a student with mild dyslexia exhibiting the symptoms of severe dyslexia. As some days may be more stressful than others, students' performance and general functioning can vary. A student may be able to perform a task well one day but not the next.

Poor working memory is often a feature of dyslexia. The physical sciences may attract dyslexic students because once they understand and can apply the basic principles of a topic, memorising a mathematical formula is less demanding than memorising the facts and providing the exposition for more discursive subjects. Drawing diagrams of animals or experiments and annotating them, often required in examinations, may be easier than describing them in words or writing an essay.

All these expressions of dyslexia may be ameliorated if the right strategies are found for, or by, a student and used appropriately. This is a joint venture on the part of a tutor and his or her student. It involves much experimentation, patience and creativity to support students in becoming aware of their own learning and finding the right approach for their study.

Something to Try: Multisensory, interactive reading for concept mapping

Modelling multisensory, interactive reading can help students to maintain attention when reading textbooks. A teacher can demonstrate this by applying the process to the building of a concept map. Concepts maps were developed by Joseph Novak in the 1950s and 1960s to support the teaching of science and their use has developed internationally (see, for example, Novak, 1990). Concept maps express the relationships and directions between ideas or elements and are related to constructivist learning, in which students build meaning together with their teacher.

The process begins by taking a chapter or the first section of a textbook, reading aloud the first sentence and then changing it to a couple of key words. These are written, in colour, on a concept map. The following sentences are treated similarly, keeping the same colour for that particular topic. A teacher then uses a different colour for each branch/topic of the concept map.

When students are reading at home they can try this method of assimilating text and transforming it for their own learning needs. Students can be encouraged to develop their own shorthand and acronyms because these are easier for them to memorise. The concept map can be used for revision purposes if the topic is to be examined.

Students will benefit from being allowed to develop their own way of producing a concept map. Sometimes students prefer to write points on Post-it notes and then build up the map by arranging the notes on an A3 sheet of paper. Other students prefer to use IT versions of concept maps and there are several types of free software available. One student said she wanted to write her essays on a 3D globe because one statement generates several connected thoughts and it was difficult to select one and maintain a single theme! This makes clear the need for the teaching of this process, and the need to help students identify key words in the concept mapping process.

Young visual learners may find help in Concept Cartoons for Science (Naylor and Keogh, 2010), used in group work to spark discussion and mutual learning. The Concept Cartoons® software images show a cartoon individual making a statement about what he sees. Other characters appear with speech bubbles, and a discussion can ensue about the issues and what the other characters are thinking. Finally all the contents of the speech bubbles are revealed. This can allow dyslexic students to become more confident in expressing their science learning. (See Useful Websites at the end of this chapter for further information.)

Case Study: Stephen

At secondary school Stephen's handwriting was a mixture of lower case cursive script and capital letters. Stephen was a gifted science student but his handwriting was a problem in chemistry classes because he sometimes wrote Co (symbol for cobalt, a metal) for CO (carbon monoxide, a noxious gas). In an examination situation, Stephen needed to write accurately and a strategy had to be found to overcome his difficulty.

It was necessary to make Stephen aware of how his handwriting would impact on his class marks and examination grades. Stephen was a visual learner so a visual periodic table was downloaded. For each of the symbols and chemical formulae that Stephen had to learn, a picture or visualisation was created by him. This helped him to memorise how the chemical was written down. For example, carbon has the symbol C and oxygen has the symbol O. Stephen had the image of a capital C made of coal 'eating' (with a wide open mouth to accentuate the fact that it is a capital) a large bubble of oxygen. Sometimes pattern recognition was easier to use; for example, formic acid HCOOH was remembered because the coal C had two bubbles of oxygen and a large bubble of hydrogen either side. Calcium carbonate (chalk) $CaCO_3$ was easier to remember because of the shape of the CaC together with the image of Ca (calcium, a metal) as a huge C next to a tiny 'a' made of chalk.

Commentary: How might a Dyslexia-friendly teacher and school support Stephen?

A Dyslexia-friendly teacher is always challenged to be creative in finding strategies to help students demonstrate their knowledge, and a Dyslexia-friendly school is sensitive to the need for this. It is important to note that the memory strategies that Stephen chooses for himself are not necessarily those that a teacher would choose for him. Stephen's choices of visualisations help him because they *are* his choices, and we must resist trying to take over this process for a student. Some students may use different strategies to overcome one difficulty; their own strategies may sound very complicated but they are easy for the individual students to use. The proof is in a student's successful memorisation.

A student may find a strategy that another student can adapt for their own purposes. An example of one student building on another's way of remembering is provided by the experience of Emily, who found it difficult to remember chemical symbols. It was suggested that she could try using some of the visualisations that Stephen had developed. Emily found visualisations difficult until she realised that a rhyming sound with the chemical in question automatically led her to a visualisation which gave her the formula. For example, 'calcium carbonate chalky agitate' then presented Emily with the image of the formula: a mental picture of chalk bubbling from acid being dropped on it (calcium carbonate effervesces when dilute hydrochloric acid is added to it).

The key to this process of intensified memorising of something when the ordinary memory process is not retaining it, lies in students tackling the issue and finding a solution. A Dyslexia-friendly teacher can facilitate this, not by imposing their own choices, but by guiding a student through this process and helping them to identify and deal with the elements in the new learning that are proving problematic.

Visual disturbance

Some individuals experience visual disturbance or Meares-Irlens Syndrome (MIS) relating to black text on white paper. Letters or words may appear in various ways: for example, they may be blurred, or may appear to shimmer, appear doubled or out of focus. In addition, a page may appear too bright and hurt the eyes of a reader. In severe cases students can have migraines if they read for more than 10 or 20 minutes.

Coloured overlays or tinted lenses can alleviate the effects and allow a student to read more easily. Visual disturbance is still being explored by researchers but Wilkins and Evans (2009) suggest that cortical hypersensitivity may be a possible cause. More recently Loew and Watson (2012) have found a possible genetic marker for MIS. It is considered that 35–40 per cent of individuals with dyslexia also have MIS. It is important to ask students how black writing on a white background appears to them.

It must be noted that issues surrounding the construct of visual stress or Meares-Irlen syndrome (also known as scotopic sensitivity syndrome) remain controversial. Studies remain divided; some educators believe that there is no real effect which helps learners to read and that in the use of coloured overlays we see a placebo effect. Against this, there are practitioners, parents and learners who insist that coloured overlays make a noticeable difference for them and that unhelpful effects of printed text are improved.

Whatever the underlying mechanism, the acquisition of literacy and mathematics skills are made more possible for learners with this experience, so if they have the same problem as Liam, below, a coloured overlay screening process can be carried out. A behavioural optometrist will undertake a detailed examination of this kind, although most coloured overlay screening takes place within a school. It is also important to make sure that assessment by an ophthalmic optician rules out any other vision problems.

For learners who consider that their visual stress is reduced by modifying the colours of a page it is worth noting the following:

- Changing the colour of the text font can also help visual stress.
- Changing the colour of a computer screen, at home and at school, can also be of benefit.
- Learners may change their colour preference over a period of time, for example after one or two years.

Student Voices: Liam

Here is the voice of a student, Liam, describing his personal experience:

> *I found it really hard to read scales and graphs in science. The lines and numbers just kept jiggling about. I have a coloured overlay now and it makes a big difference.*
> (Liam aged 10)

What might a Dyslexia-friendly teacher learn from this?

1. Students who are not very responsive to questions about graphs may understand what is being asked of them but not be able to read the scales. It is important that we do not make assumptions but enquire gently, perhaps outside of the class lesson, in order to determine why they may not be able to answer questions of this kind.

2. We need to ask any student, of whatever age, who is struggling with reading what black writing on white paper looks like to them. MIS needs to be addressed before any possibility of a specific learning difficulty is considered.

3. If possible we should always use off-white paper which reduces glare from the page.

4. Some students require different paper tints to others, and we also need to be aware that some students might require alternative coloured papers for handouts and for writing. Providing tinted paper when students ask for it constitutes a 'reasonable adjustment'.

5. It is useful to have a stock of coloured overlays or Eye Rulers, so that all students can experiment with using them.

Information and Communication Technology: Predictive text and text-to-speech

Some students find predictive text (where part of a word is typed and the software supplies the rest) easy to use, as they can recognise whether the word selected is correct. However, a student with more severe spelling difficulties may find predictive text impossible to use correctly. In this case text-to-speech software, for example, TextHELP Read and Write, can help. The Texthelp Ltd website provides a free 30-day trial. A student can highlight a word and the various homophones are defined and inserted in a sentence so the correct word can be selected as it is exemplified in context.

If a student has problems with proofreading essays then text-to-speech can be helpful, because a student can hear what is written on the screen and see or hear whether the word used was the intended one. For some students text-to-speech is the end process of dictating words via speech recognition; the computer 'reads' back the text that has been written.

The Gunning FOG Index, developed by Robert Gunning in the 1950s, is a readability tool to check whether our writing is too complex to be easily comprehensible. It differs from the readability measure in Chapter 2 by calculating, for a 100-word extract, the number of sentences and the number of long words. The resulting figure or 'index' judges the number of years of formal education required to comprehend the meaning of a text when reading it for the first time. While not all long words are difficult, and not all short words are easy, the FOG index can tell us when we are being overly complex. For general readability the index needs to be around the figure eight (representing eight years of formal education). There are a number of free Gunning FOG calculators available through the Internet.

Homework: Homework and science clubs, and online science homework

Although homework is generally intended for completion at home, a Dyslexia-friendly teacher may find it more constructive to support a dyslexic student in school at lunchtime or after school by arrangement. Where a piece of work is to be completed after a lesson a dyslexic student may require more support for reading or compiling charts, graphs or scales. For maximum learning to occur such work might be usefully completed with teaching support in school. Homework clubs provide a context where dyslexic learners can be supported in this way.

At the same time, after-school science clubs can be instrumental in enthusing and motivating students, and helping them to enjoy their learning. Science clubs can promote an experimental approach to learning, and it is with this in mind that we suggest the club approach to undertaking on-line science homework. There are a number of such programs available, with the website of Oxford University Press offering samples of GCSE Science homework.

Online homework programs mark themselves and provide immediate feedback to show a student how they have performed. Students enjoy them, and they also save time for teachers in setting and marking homework. Online homework programs are not necessarily constructed with Dyslexia-friendly methods in mind; although they can use such aids as pictures and missing-word procedures, they also use a great deal of text. We suggest then that such programs could be used collaboratively, in the context of a science or a homework club, with the guidance of a teacher. It would not matter if marks were gained together, unless the purpose of the homework was to judge individual attainment; collaborative learning can be rewarding in its own right.

Homework can often consist of writing the discussion part of an experiment performed earlier in class. In order to help a student move from notes or data taken in a practical session, a scaffolding technique, whereby direct questions are asked and responded to in simple sentences, may help the student write in a linear fashion. Figure 7.1 is a photocopiable resource which can help students formulate their ideas and write them down in a logical way.

Revision: Visual learning

Visual learners may find visualisations helpful, particularly in conjunction with a visual number system. If the student finds concept maps good for learning, a visual number system, whereby each number is visualised, can help. For example, the number 1 may look like a candle, so an association can be made between the candle and the fact to be remembered. Verbal learners may find mnemonics helpful and visual learners can add a picture to the words or sounds the mnemonic prompts.

Pattern recognition can be helpful in memorising formulae. For example, if a student is comfortable with the alphabet then the formula:

$$\text{density} = \text{mass/volume}$$

gives the relevant symbols in alphabetical order:

$$d = m/v$$

Scaffolding template for writing experiments	
What is the question you are asking?	
How are you going to test it?	
What equipment do you need?	
What did you do?	
What happened?	
How was your question answered?	
What can you do now? Are there more questions to answer?	

Figure 7.1 A scaffolding template for writing experiments

Calculations, worked examples and proofs require overlearning – they need to be repeated and any variations rehearsed in order to develop automaticity and speed so that the minimum amount of time is used for this task in examination situations. Visualisations can help to support this process.

Five steps in moving to a Dyslexia-friendly approach to science

Recognise that a student who is verbally knowledgeable about science in the classroom and yet not able to reflect this in her/his written work may need specific help.

↓

Provide examples of scaffolding written work to the whole class, so that all students may benefit from this strategy of presenting work in a logical fashion.

↓

Encourage experimental ability and develop practical skills as a positive affirmation of students who find written work arduous.

↓

Share scaffolding of science written work with all disciplines across the school.

↓

Apply these strategies across all the sciences.

Whole-school and whole-class strategies for a science focus

Table 7.1 considers school and class strategies that support science teaching and learning in relation to dyslexia.

Table 7.1 Whole-school and whole-class strategies for a science focus

	Early Years	**Primary**	**Secondary**	**Tertiary**
Whole-school strategy	The importance of science is reflected in policy and practice. There is a process to evaluate students' ability in science. A child's natural curiosity is harnessed to explore the natural world.	School policy for science teaching reflects Dyslexia-friendly methods. There is a system in place for noticing and identifying students who have a practical aptitude for science but cannot write down their work.	The subject-focused curriculum allows alternative ways of recording and demonstrating knowledge. Practical expertise is recognised. Where a child has good practical ability but cannot write down what s/he knows accompanied perhaps with behavioural difficulties, there is assessment for dyslexia and appropriate teaching is put in place.	Strategy reflects possible late identification of dyslexia and makes arrangements and adjustments accordingly. All staff understand that dyslexic students may find the practicals and lectures exhausting and be prepared to give an extension to deadlines for the submission of written work.
Whole-class strategy	Teaching encourages a spirit of enquiry and observation which can be used to channel a child's natural enthusiasm and imagination. Teacher gives children the space to formulate their own conclusions but may provide hints as to what is occurring.	Teaching encourages accurate use of scientific terms in writing and diagrams using Dyslexia-friendly approaches. Discussion and working in pairs or groups is encouraged so students with ability can enthuse other students.	Teaching encourages written enquiry and creativity as well as subject knowledge. The use of multi-sensory teaching and learning continues, including discussions and working in pairs.	Teachers look for a discrepancy between verbal knowledge and marks in written assessments. Multi-sensory teaching is still a feature of the classroom. Group science projects enable dyslexic students to maximise strengths.

Useful websites

- Concept Cartoons® for Science: http://www.millgatehouse.co.uk/science/ccs. This website offers examples of the Concept Cartoons ® used in: Naylor, S. and Keogh, B. (2010) *Concept Cartoons in Science Education* (rev. edn). Sandbach: Millgate House Education. The website lists details of other science-based resources using the Concept Cartoon® approach. These include interactive CD-Roms together with paper editions.
- British Broadcasting Corporation (BBC) 2012: *Schools Home page*. This gives access to Science sites for ages 4–11, 11–16, and 16+. While not aimed directly at accommodating dyslexia, resources on this website have high visual content. The resources generate practical activities for parents and teachers, and these could be adjusted to incorporate further Dyslexia-friendly practices. Available online at: http://www.bbc.co.uk/schools/.
- The Association for Science Education has resources for teaching science, including articles on working with students who experience dyslexia or other learning difficulties. Available online at: http://www.ase.org.uk/home/.

Further reading

Barrass, R. (2002) *Scientists Must Write: A Guide to Better Writing for Scientists, Engineers and Students*. London: Routledge.

McKissock, C. (2009) *Great Ways to Learn Anatomy and Physiology*. Basingstoke: Palgrave Macmillan.

Peer, L. and Reid, G. (2001) *Dyslexia-Successful Inclusion in the Secondary School*. London: David Fulton, published in association with the British Dyslexia Association; this publication has chapters on 'Dyslexia and physics' (by Pam Holmes), 'Dyslexia and biology' (by Christine A. Howlett) and 'Dyslexia and general science' (by Vicky Hunter).

8

Dyslexia and creativity

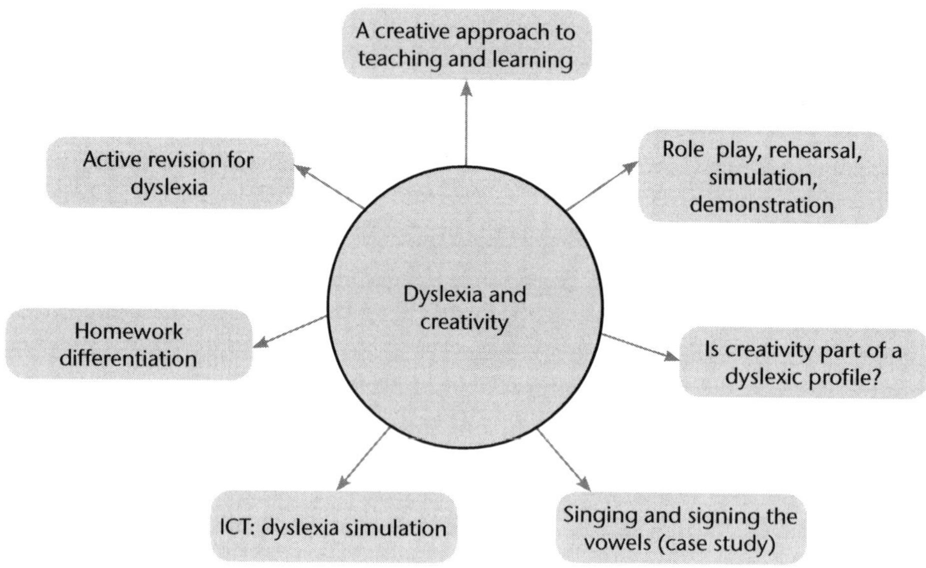

If dyslexia is a 'fuzzy' term, so too is creativity. The Robinson Report on creativity (National Advisory Committee on Creative and Cultural Education, 1999) noted the elusiveness of definitions, considering that there were different definitions for different contexts. The Committee ultimately defined creativity as:

> Imaginative activity fashioned so as to produce outcomes that are both original and of value. (NACCCE, 1999: 30)

While creativity can be acknowledged by governments for the dimensions it can add to human lives, there is a developing policy focus about what creative, arts-based experience can bring to increasing educational outcomes, students' interest in schooling, problem-solving and teamwork. The good practice points below give some pointers about how creativity and arts-based activities can support dyslexic learners, calling on teachers' own creativity.

Good Practice Points: A creative approach to teaching and learning

Creative Dyslexia-friendly teachers understand that:

1. Creativity is wider than arts-based activity; it encompasses thinking, problem-solving and the generation of ideas.
2. A teacher's own creativity can be explored and exploited in developing pedagogical experience.
3. Learning can be through creative means. Being able to use their creativity may be a lifeline for dyslexic students.
4. Quality can be developed by encouraging creativity in students, making creative activity available for teaching and learning, and encouraging students to use creative activity to demonstrate skills and knowledge.
5. We put in a 'step' when the move from one concept, skill or item of knowledge to another is too big, asking, 'What can I do to make this task accessible?' A 'step' can use creative approaches and media, moving dyslexic learners away from failure and lack of confidence.
6. Teaching can be reinvigorated by the challenge of teaching and learning without recourse to reading and writing, e.g. by using drawing, demonstration, role play or rehearsal. This offers dyslexic pupils the chance to work without disadvantage. It also reminds us how much we rely upon literacy.
7. Learners can be encouraged to see their work as an investigative process where unexpected results ('error') are not a cause of blame. Learners can be asked to try the activity again, seeing if, with guidance, they can produce a better result – in a creative, solution-focused process.
8. Access to different materials and modes of expression widens opportunities for success, bearing in mind that some dyslexic learners may have difficulty in gross or fine motor control.
9. Quality of outcome is more likely when good quality materials are provided for students' creative activity.
10. In creative activity, some people have a loud creative 'voice', others a quiet one. We need to recognise both.

An international interest in creativity

There is no doubt that many nations are concerned about the role and place of creativity in the national educational project, using the term creativity in a wider sense and reflecting an international trend whereby the capacity to think and act creatively and innovatively are linked to economic development. Tienken and Zhao consider that creativity is important to enable the USA to retain its character as a 'nimble economy' (2010: 3). Tan (2010) describes efforts to broaden the Singaporean educational curriculum to allow for the development of creativity and innovation, as these are seen as helping to retain high levels of development and manufacturing achievement. In Australia Gillard (2010) describes the K-10 curriculum as embedding ten capabilities, one of which is creativity, again used in a context that stretches beyond arts subjects, embodying the skills needed across the whole range of the curriculum. There is an awareness of industries centred around creative activity and a turn towards positioning creative activity within a cultural context (Henley 2012).

Something to Try: Teaching and learning through role play, rehearsal, simulation and demonstration

For learners who experience dyslexia there are advantages in having creative activities incorporated into an existing programme. Performance can be used to make a valuable teaching point. While not everyone will want to be a performer, everyone can be a receptive audience member.

To explore the teaching and learning potential of performance such as in role play, rehearsal, simulation and demonstration, we:

1. Prepare our exercise. For example we may ask students to show us a family argument or we may ask them to show us the structure of a sonnet . . .
2. Say that we are going to ask for volunteers to demonstrate to the class through performing, i.e. to show the class a live 'picture' of something.
3. Acknowledge that some people will not want to do this and they will not be pressed to do something they don't want to do.
4. Tell them what the job is so that the prospect is not too worrisome.
5. Acknowledge that some will be OK with it and ask for volunteers.
6. Identify 4–6 'actors'. Some may need to be coaxed!
7. Give them the script/plan/ props and say how long we are going to let it run for and that we are going to stop it at the right time.
8. Send them away to another room or corner to sort out what they are going to do.
9. Ask the others to clear a space and arrange a performing area visible to all. Tables may need to be moved.
10. Find a moment to tell the performers they might make their performance a bit 'larger than life' so that the audience may understand and so that it is seen happening in the acting space and not in the actor's heads.
11. Tell actors that they will need to keep acting even when attention is not primarily on them – they should not let the character drop.
12. Bring the performers into the performing area when they are ready.
13. Tell the audience, before beginning, they *must not laugh*, this is not entertainment, it is learning by another method than the ones they usually use.
14. Ask the performers not to start until everyone is ready. This will be when all are quiet and attending to the performers.
15. Say 'OK, start now' when all are focused on the actors.
16. Step into the scenario and call a halt when it is time to tell the actors to stop – that is, when we judge they have done enough to make the point.
17. Lead the audience in a round of applause straight away, as a 'thank you' for what the performers have done.
18. Go on to discuss the points made, perhaps in groups (we are not providing a critique of the performance).
19. Allow the performers to contribute their experience and understanding of what they have done.
20. Leave the room as we found it.

Anyone who doubts how far this process can be taken, might find it interesting to view the examples of dance performance explanations at the higher level of study found in the 'Dance Your PhD' competition (website address is shown at the end of the chapter). The scale of the prizes show that this is a concept that, while entertaining, is taken seriously.

Is creativity part of a dyslexia profile?

A discussion of creativity in relation to dyslexia owes much to Tim West, whose influential 1997 book *In the Mind's Eye* focused upon gifted individuals working in the sciences who also experienced dyslexia. West's view was that his subjects had visual-spatial strengths linked with their dyslexia and with their capacity to innovate. This may have had a strong influence upon the view that people with dyslexia benefited from a better-developed creative ability. However, it is also possible that West's individual subjects fell within the group of people who experience 'dual exceptionality' (Brody and Mills, 1997), also described as 'twice exceptional' or '2e' (Jackson, 2010). That is to say, since we now consider that dyslexia is not characterised by intellect, West's group may have been as much identified by their giftedness as by their dyslexia.

In an editorial note in the journal *Dyslexia* in 2009, Michael Thompson, calling for further research, refers to the 'received wisdom' that people who experience dyslexia are inherently creative, especially in the areas of visual art and design. Experiential and cognitive research can be found exploring this area, along with assertions that dyslexic learners have a particular visual-spatial strength. Alexander-Passe (2010), investigating, concludes that there is a lack of consistent evidence to this effect, although the idea that people who experience dyslexia have compensatory talents is valued by some.

If there is evidence that there might be a higher than expected proportion of dyslexic learners among creative individuals, Bacon and Handley (2010) outline a number of reasons why this might be so:

- an evolutionary bias toward visual communication, reflected in brain organisation, with the characteristics of dyslexia not evident and of no consequence until uncovered by the demand for a wholly literate society;
- a case of learners choosing areas that do not rely on their weaker skills in literacy;
- a co-occurrence of the two characteristics (dyslexia and creativity) that does not represent a causal relationship;
- the emotional as well as functional impact of dyslexia leading to the development of alternative (visual) strategies;
- a misreading of the discrepancy between unaffected functioning in visual and creative areas compared with impaired functioning in literacy areas.

This is a useful analysis, worth exploring in full because all these differing perspectives may be found in views about dyslexia. If there is a higher than expected prevalence of people experiencing dyslexia in the creative arts, Wolff (2010) argues that they should be considered as a subgroup.

Case Study: Jed and Rona

Jed and Rona's teacher worked hard to help them to remember when to use long and short vowel sounds, but the knowledge did not seem to be retained. The SENCO suggested that the class teacher should intensify the input by using multisensory methods including singing and the use of signs and movements. This sounded a little far-fetched to the class teacher but she asked for a demonstration.

The SENCO showed how she used hand signs and a sung tone for the long vowel sounds. Short vowel sounds (the letter names) were spoken, but since the long sounds were sung, there was a clear difference between long and short vowel sounds. At the same time, the teacher moved her hands away from her body, indicating that the sound was elongated. She had a different sign for each vowel's long sound, giving a clue to the vowel by suggesting its shape.*

The SENCO explained that, having practised this so they were familiar with the signs, students then scrutinised words, including mute 'e' words, which took the long vowel sound. The students had to identify the vowel and say whether it was sung or not. If it was sung (long) they would do the sign and sing the sound before they attempted the word. Singing helped to ensure that students got the right sound because they had to sustain the longer breath.

Beginning with Jed and Rona, the teacher found that this became a method for the whole class, even when they could already distinguish between long and short vowel sounds. The class enjoyed singing the notes and doing the movements extending the 'sounds' away from them. Jed was rather embarrassed about singing so his teacher gave him options – to mime while singing the note in his head, and to demonstrate to her alone that he was doing it correctly.

Jed and Rona's confidence and skill was increased by the additional practice, and by the obvious enjoyment of everybody else taking part. Everyone became very skilled at distinguishing words using long and short vowel sounds, particularly where there was a mute 'e' involved.

*For 'A' she made a triangle with touching index fingers and touching thumbs which looked like the point of an uppercase 'A'. For 'E' she used the three middle fingers (without thumb and little finger) sideways like an uppercase 'E', then brushing the three fingers with the same three fingers of the other hand as she sang its long vowel sound. For 'O' she made an 'O' shape by enclosing index finger to thumb and moving it away from her mouth as she sang the long vowel sound. 'I' had a raised index finger which the SENCO pointed to herself, then moving her finger away as she sang the long vowel sound for 'I'. 'U' had raised thumb and index finger, with the other three fingers folded down). This made a U shape which the SENCO stroked with her other hand, then tipped it so that it pointed at the student ('you').

Commentary: How might a Dyslexia-friendly teacher and school support Jed and Rona?

A Dyslexia-friendly school will offer opportunities for the exchange of information and techniques of the kind used with Jed and Rona; these are not just the province of the SENCO. Not everyone feels comfortable with singing, but the singing does not have to be of a high standard to be useful; a Dyslexia-friendly teacher will sing if and when it helps. Schools and practitioners can be pleased that the whole class enjoyed the activity and benefited from it, even though not everyone needed that differentiation.

The stimulus needed to help Jed and Rona to differentiate between short and long vowels needed to be stronger and more vivid than was first thought. It used multisensory methods and small steps, it connected the learning of the long vowels to the short vowels and carried on for longer. This level of understanding should be shared by all school practitioners. When sharing information of this kind, a Dyslexia-friendly school needs also to share information with its practitioners about how to 'fade' a stimulus, revisiting it now and then, so that the intervention is not administered and then left behind.

Creative Voices: Mike Juggins

Here are the words of Mike Juggins, a well-known artist:

> *My dyslexia is the source of my creativity and a massive part of who I am . . .*
>
> *I have also worked as a community artist, educator and film-maker in many educational and social settings. Because I was that 'slow learner' I guess I always aim to make things as multisensory as possible. I believe that accessible information motivates success and always encourage others to* ***focus on ability****.*
>
> *I continue to devote some of my time to these issues in the belief that the right intervention can help people turn their lives around. However, I went to university to develop my painting, the physical visual and emotional joy I get from painting is pure beauty to my soul.* ***Painting is my high place*** *and at times I guess that I use it as a safety valve from the pressure of being a dyslexic in a text-based society. It's something I need to do daily.* (M.J., artist) (Emphasis the artist's)

What might a Dyslexia-friendly teacher learn from this?

1. The part that creative activity can play in a person's life is valued.
2. In teaching creatively a Dyslexia-friendly teacher is not alone; others share his/her values and appreciate his/her skills.
3. Dyslexia is becoming more widely discussed and understood through the willingness of people to share their dyslexia experience.
4. The ability to envisage how to employ multisensory methods is important.
5. Protecting students' confidence when learning literacy skills is crucial. A Dyslexia-friendly teacher understands that dyslexia may be a characteristic but need not be a drawback or the source of an insurmountable lack of confidence.

Information and Communication Technology: Dyslexia simulations

In 2000, Margaret Rooms expressed the view that 'Accessing the Internet for information will become more Dyslexia-Friendly' (272). She was correct: there is predictive text for typing into a search window, and there are codes of practice and protocols governing access. On certain web pages we can find opportunities to change the font and to change the background colour. On the other hand Internet pages have proliferated, and sometimes web pages are constructed in a way that is confusing, especially where animations are involved.

One way in which the Internet has become more dyslexia-aware is in the number of pages and recordings given over to people explaining and illustrating their dyslexia experience, and seeking to inform others about dyslexia. Among these are a number of websites that provide simulations of dyslexia, which are useful for personal reflection or staff training. Wadlington et al. (2008) report good results in raising practitioner awareness using a simulation kit from the Northern California Branch of the International Dyslexia Association (NCBIDA). The kit, now called Experience Dyslexia, is available for purchase, but a useful 'trailer' is available on YouTube under the title 'PEN Speakers Series Review: Experience Dyslexia October 27 2011'.

A different approach to simulating dyslexia is also found on YouTube under the title 'What is it like to have dyslexia? Animations and Illustrations'. Whether or not a dyslexic student's dyslexia experience is replicated here, this short film is thought-provoking for practitioners. However, looking at a film is not sufficient to gain a clear understanding of dyslexia. Wadlington et al.'s research showed that undertaking tasks that aim to replicate the experience of dyslexia – such as writing with the non-dominant hand – help to create understanding.

Homework: Differentiation

In the literature about homework we find descriptions of optimum situations in which all homework is meaningful. It extends learners, is individually devised for learners and is negotiated with learners, and in the homework task learners are helped by parents. The reality may be different, and for dyslexic learners homework is particularly problematic. Fatigued students may return home from school burdened with negativity and low self-esteem, facing a long evening containing the same sort of tasks with which they have struggled all day. Riddick (2010) describes the efforts made by parents to support their children, but some parents of dyslexic students will be dyslexic themselves, and may not be able to help as much as the literature presumes. Parents and practitioners alike may, without meaning to, criticise and focus on negatives.

The likelihood is that homework will remain a regular part of the educational experience, so we need to think about making it more manageable for dyslexic students. While it may be possible to negotiate the individual adjustments to which dyslexic students are entitled, the reality of a busy school with different subjects and competing claims on teacher's time and attention, means that there is only one real way of making homework meaningful and manageable for dyslexic learners, and that is to differentiate it.

One straightforward way of differentiating homework is to centre it on time rather than content (Vatterott, 2010), so that the homework subject ceases when a time limit has been reached, for example a student may be asked to write as much as they can in 30 minutes. For learning spellings, the word list may be stratified – everyone learns three, possibly key, words, but students can learn five if they wish and ten if they want to challenge themselves.

In devising lesson plans and schemes of work, teachers are likely to be familiar with differentiating class-work tasks, and this planning should extend to homework. Some homework may be concerned with finishing tasks or doing a textbook exercise, nevertheless there could be key points through the term where the homework is more carefully differentiated.

Helpful guidance can be found in Cathy Vatterott's (2010) article '5 Hallmarks of Good Homework'. The author focuses upon the key characteristics of Purpose, Efficiency, Ownership, Competence and Aesthetic appeal. Her recommendations for improving the quality of homework are valuable for all students, and include the importance of differentiation in making homework manageable. Making such changes will build up a bank of resources for teachers' future use, and will provide more interesting, manageable and successful homework experiences for dyslexic students.

Revision: Active revision for dyslexia

There is a great deal of advice about revision available on the Internet, and much of it is aimed at learners who experience dyslexia. There are many useful ideas. Unfortunately this advice is communicated through words, necessitating reading, and invariably it suggests organisation through writing. Sometimes the text does not conform to dyslexia-accessible values, undermining its worth by making it extremely difficult to read for a dyslexic student. Such well-meaning efforts overlook the very problems experienced by dyslexic learners, namely difficulties with reading, writing, spelling (which make the act of written expression problematic), sequencing and memory.

Much of the revision advice is in favour of *active revision* – this involves using and reorganising the information to be revised. Such advice employs a suitably active vocabulary inviting students to select, interpret, find themes and so on. However, perhaps the key word for dyslexic students is 'manage' – the whole question is how to manage revision when revision techniques themselves are problematic and the anxiety and the effort load are doubled.

To help dyslexic students to revise, we need to think about the characteristics of dyslexia. This means that, for a student, the knowledge, understanding and ideas may be in place but may not find easy expression in written form. For a dyslexic student, sequencing according to a pre-decided linear progression may not be so obvious, either in following content or in creating a written argument. It may mean that safe vocabulary and simplified expression are used, accompanied by written work that is slower than the pace of thinking. The resulting argument may leap from place to place, with one sentence addressing a topic and the rest of the information in the student's head.

Knowing this about dyslexia, here are some ideas for active revision that may help a dyslexic student to manage their revision:

- We start with a graphic representation of the topic – a Mind Map® or spidergram, with the topic in the middle. Someone else scribes this while a student talks about the key points in the topic, in any order. The diagram needs to be simple without too many points – three to five key points will probably be sufficient. Pictures can be used if it is easier. Pavey et al. (2010) note the example of a student who used Widgit software© for note-taking and revision.
- A dyslexic student copies this out until they can do it with their eyes actually shut, and they practise this now and again (they can transfer it to rough paper when they get into the examination room).
- Later, revising the revision, a student can add 1–3 bullet points to each key point. Once again, we are resisting the inclusion of too much information.

- The information in the graphic diagram can be used to complete the daisy shape (see Figure 8.1), answering, with a word or two, the questions: What? Who? When? Where? Why? How? What's important? What if . . . ? The 'petals' can be done in any order, and some may be omitted if they seem irrelevant. The 'What if . . . ?' question encourages thinking to widen, and prompts questioning of the material.
- The analysis can be transferred from the daisy shape to the linear diagram in Figure 8.1, giving a sense of sequence.

By the time a dyslexic student has done all this for a topic, they have gone over the material several times with the minimum of writing, so that both content and sequence have a better opportunity for being sustained.

Five steps in moving to staff and student creativity for dyslexia

Use imagination and creativity to make teaching stimuli bigger, bolder, more multisensory, and to connect them to other learning.

↓

Make good quality creative materials and media available.

↓

Celebrate and value students' creativity.

↓

Maintain an aesthetically pleasing learning environment.

↓

Link literacy to artistic and creative endeavour of all kinds.

Whole-school and whole-class strategies for developing and applying creativity

Table 8.1 considers school and class strategies that support the development and application of creativity when working with learners who experience dyslexia.

Daisy shape

What..

Who..

When..

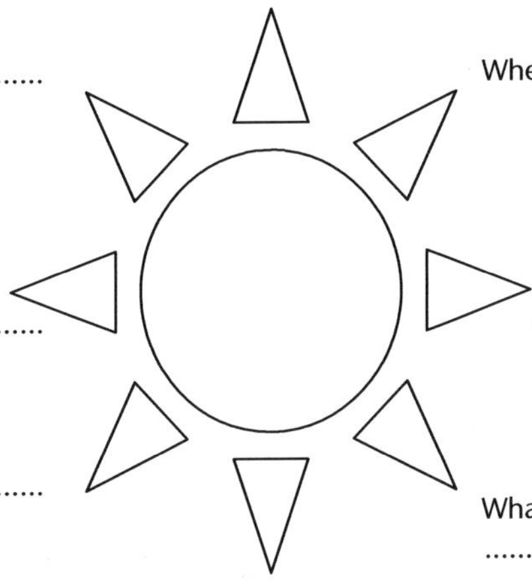

Where..

Why ....

How..

What's important

....

What if..

Linear

Topic

1. What ....
2. Who ....
3. When ....
4. Where ....
5. Why ....
6. How ....
7. What's important..
8. What if ....

Figure 8.1 Active revision templates

Table 8.1 Whole-school and whole-class strategies for developing and applying creativity

	Early years	**Primary**	**Secondary**	**Tertiary**
Whole-school strategy	Policy encourages exploration of a wide range of creative experiences, both for their own sake and for stimulating literacy teaching. Schools do not economise by using cheap materials or doing 'creative' activities based on using up left-over materials.	Policy encourages use of a variety of creative methods and media in recording and expression. School resists the temptation to base the great majority of learning upon literacy-focused tasks, enabling students to express their knowledge by using creative media.	School demonstrates that creative activity is valued. It does not place all sense of worth upon literacy achievement, although literacy development continues to be of importance. Strategy is to place learners in groups and settings where their creative ability can be an asset to a group, rather than placing them in lower ability settings.	Strategy is to plan assignments that enable students to express their knowledge by using creative media. There is guidance on how to mark these, e.g. presentation, poster. Staff in all subjects notice when learners are relying on a 'safe' vocabulary, and encourage them to move beyond this by employing creative methods.
Whole-class strategy	There is a clear goal for creative activity. Singing is used to encourage rhyming, rhythmic clapping and percussion are used to encourage hearing a beat (aiding later syllabification), acting is used to encourage narrative and sequence, visual media are used to encourage explanation, story-telling and knowledge-sharing.	Good quality creative opportunities are offered using a wide range of media. Singing is used to remember literacy facts and mnemonics; music is used to emphasise rhythm and beat, and to create a sense of progression; performance, role play and rehearsal are used to demonstrate explanation and knowledge sharing; visual media are used to depict knowledge and understanding in a different way to writing.	Students who have creative skills are encouraged to develop them, in visual or performing arts, in thinking, discussion and problem-solving. Students are not made to forgo these activities because literacy or other work is unfinished.	Mature creative thinking, problem-solving and use of creative materials are valued and respected while literacy development continues. The development of literacy skills makes use of a variety of visual and performance media and methods in order to reinforce literacy learning points. This is done with the agreement of students in order to avoid any possible embarrassment.

Useful websites

- Mike Juggins' work and discussion: http://mikejuggins.moonfruit.com
- The Dance Your PhD Contest 2012: http://gonzolabs.org/dance/
- The Yale Centre for Dyslexia and Creativity has tips for educators (top ribbon): http://dyslexia.yale.edu/

Further reading

Alexander-Passe, N. (ed.) (2010) *Dyslexia and Creativity: Investigations from Differing Perspectives.* New York: Nova Science Publishers.

Kiziewicz, M. and Biggs, I. (eds) (2007) *CASCADE: Creativity Across Science, Arts, Dyslexia, Education.* Available online at http://www.bath.ac.uk/.

Vatterott, C. (2010) '5 hallmarks of good homework', *Education Leadership,* 68 (1): 10–15.

Appendix

A Dyslexia-friendly school – a practitioner's guide

Self-Evaluation/Audit Tool: How Dyslexia-friendly Is My Classroom?

Date: ....

Part 1: The Dyslexia-friendly Classroom

(*Photocopiable*)

A. Text resources available in the classroom	**Never**	**Sometimes** (less than 50%)	**Middling** (about 50%)	**Usually** (more than 50%)	**Always**
1. Reading age of text is checked for accessibility					
2. Interest level of text is appropriate to age range					
3. Font is clearly distinguishable, with rounded shape, preferably size 14 pt					
4. Photocopies are clean and clear					
5. Text is in small groups: 5 lines maximum					
6. There are frequent subheadings, shown in bold					
7. Off-white or tinted paper is used					
8. Blocks of text are clearly separated					
9. Headings/subheadings are clearly separated from text					
10. Diagrams and illustrations are used					
11. Diagrams and illustrations give same information as, or relate to, text					
12. Diagrams and illustrations are near relevant text					
Total					

B. Focused Dyslexia-friendly teaching to support literacy skills	**Never**	**Sometimes** (less than 50%)	**Middling** (about 50%)	**Usually** (more than 50%)	**Always**
1. Spelling tests are short and differentiated					
2. Phonics skills are taught visually and aurally					
3. Mnemonics are used to help students remember spellings					
4. Cloze procedures are used to vary writing tasks					
5. Writing frames are used to support writing tasks					
6. Miscue analysis is used to gain understanding of students' reading difficulties					
7. Texts are broken down into small chunks					
8. Instructions are broken down into small parts					
9. Sequencing is taught as a skill					
10. SMART targets are used in planning teaching and learning					
11. 'Concrete' literacy targets are used in planning teaching and learning					
12. Texts are given to students ahead of time for practice purposes					
Total					

C. Classroom arrangements	**Never**	**Sometimes** (less than 50%)	**Middling** (about 50%)	**Usually** (more than 50%)	**Always**
1. Care is taken so that students with possible dyslexia see and hear the teacher clearly					
2. Students experiencing possible dyslexia have opportunities to work with their peers					
3. Students experiencing possible dyslexia have opportunities to work in a quiet area					
4. Students experiencing possible dyslexia have opportunities to display their understanding					
5. Items in classrooms are clearly labelled					
6. Labels include languages other than English where appropriate					
7. Practitioners' handwriting is clear					
8. Avoided: rapid change in classroom layout					
9. Visual displays conform to text resource guidelines (section A above)					
10. Students experiencing possible dyslexia can use a computer to produce class work					
11. Students experiencing possible dyslexia can use a computer to produce homework					
12. Relevant literacy apparatus is available for students to use if they feel the need					
13. Coloured overlays are available if students benefit from them					
14. Students who request tinted paper may have it					
15. Practical apparatus is available regardless of age					
Total					

D. Affective aspects	**Never**	**Sometimes** (less than 50%)	**Middling** (about 50%)	**Usually** (more than 50%)	**Always**
1. Practitioners know and use a range of teaching and learning styles (particularly visual, auditory or kinaesthetic)					
2. Practitioners challenge students to use different learning styles, in a manageable way					
3. Practitioners know their own preferred individual learning styles (their comfort zone)					
4. Practitioners challenge themselves to move outside their own comfort zone					
6. Avoided: judgements of laziness					
7. Avoided: the giving of punishment for small amounts of work					
8. Students are praised and reassured even for a small amount of work					
9. Students reading in front of class is voluntary (rather than by adult selection)					
10. Students writing on the board or in front of class is voluntary					
11. Students spelling aloud or on the board is voluntary					
12. There is a reward system in class					
13. Rewards can be achieved by all the students in the class					
14. Learning tasks consider and deal with emotional issues first					
15. Care is taken that students are not teased for literacy difficulties					
16. Care is taken that extra work time does not eliminate enjoyed activities (break, golden time)					
17. Care is taken to protect students' feelings					
Total					

E. Classroom interactions	**Never**	**Sometimes** (less than 50%)	**Middling** (about 50%)	**Usually** (more than 50%)	**Always**
1. Practitioners' concerns about students' literacy are respected					
2. Parents' and carers' concerns about their students' literacy are respected					
3. Students' concerns about their own literacy are respected					
4. Avoided: use of practitioner loud, raised voice (it destroys thinking)					
5. Home-school diaries include praise					
6. Classroom practitioners meet with English as additional language specialist(s)					
7. Classroom practitioners meet with dyslexia specialist(s)					
8. Classroom practitioners meet with speech and language specialist(s)					
9. There are opportunities to observe classroom interactions when a child experiences literacy difficulties					
10. Avoided: ranking of students according to their literacy skills					
11. Attendance levels of students experiencing possible or actual dyslexia are high					
Total					

F. General Dyslexia-friendly teaching and learning	**Never**	**Sometimes** (less than 50%)	**Middling** (about 50%)	**Usually** (more than 50%)	**Always**
Teaching					
1. Instructions are clearly identified on the page or board					
2. Statements are clear, without ambiguity (check with another person)					
3. Explanations are repeated, in different ways, as students require					
4. Timescale of a task is clearly stated, supportively (see 5 below)					
5. Extra time is allowed for students to finish written work if necessary					
6. Length of product (how much you want the students to do) is clearly stated					
7. Length of product makes allowances for dyslexia					
8. Subject-specific words are linked to clear concepts					
9. Practitioner talking is reduced (maximum 10 mins)					
10. Board copying is reduced (maximum 5 lines)					
11. Handouts are available to reduce board copying (following guidelines in section A)					
12. Input is given in small 'chunks'					
13. Input takes account of multisensory learning – visual, auditory, kinaesthetic					
14. VAK stimuli and tasks are close together					
15. Teaching uses diagrams and illustrations					
16. Teaching uses bullet points and lists					
17. Colour is used as an identifier: colour coding, highlighting, colour blocks for focus					
18. New concepts are linked to previous concepts					
19. New techniques are linked to previous techniques					
20. Any changes acknowledge what students say about how best they learn					
21. Assessment/marking criteria are clearly stated, including those for alternative formats					
Learning					
22. Students' output uses diagrams and illustrations					
23. Students' output uses bullet points and numbered lists					
24. Students can use alternative means of recording, e.g. poster, tape, ICT					
25. Students are allowed (or encouraged) to do the picture first					
26. Students are asked how best they learn					
27. Students are allowed to ask questions					
28. Students' output is judged on quality and content					
Total					

Self-Evaluation/Audit Tool: How Dyslexia-friendly Is My Classroom?

Part 2: The Dyslexia-friendly Classroom within the School Setting

	I Think No	Unsure	I Think Yes
1. There is a school marking policy in use			
2. There is a school reading policy in use			
3. There is a school handwriting policy in use			
4. There is a school spelling policy in use			
5. There is a shared understanding of the point at which concerns about a child's reading, spelling or handwriting are discussed with parents or carers			
6. There is a shared understanding about the point at which concerns about a child's reading, spelling or handwriting are discussed with the SENCO			
7. There is a shared understanding about the point at which dyslexia-specific assessments are carried out in school for a child			
8. There is a shared understanding about the point at which advice external to the school should be sought when it is suspected that a child may experience dyslexia			
9. There are up-to-date dyslexia assessment materials for use within school			
10. There is access to at least one dyslexia-specific program within the school for use in helping students who experience dyslexia			
11. There are Dyslexia-friendly books in the school library with age-appropriate interest, but with text that is of a reduced amount and accessible, for students who find reading difficult			
12. Dyslexia-friendly books are easy for readers to find			
13. Dyslexia-friendly books are indicated in a way that is not embarrassing for students			
14. The presence of Dyslexia-friendly books in the library is checked by eye, not just by catalogue			
15. There are dyslexia support ICT programs within school			
Total			

To conclude the self-evaluation process:

1. Which do you think are the most important out of all the self-evaluation items?

....

....

....

2. How do you think your classroom is doing in relation to those items? What are the classroom strengths and weaknesses?

....

....

....

3. As a result of undertaking this self-evaluation, what 3 priority targets would you now set for the coming year (or shorter period)?

(1) ....

(2) ....

(3) ....

4. Are there any further comments or reminders for when you look back on this evaluation?

....

....

....

Date of this evaluation: .... Date of next evaluation: ....

Evaluation carried out by: ....

References

Alexander, R. (2003) *Talk for Learning, the First Year*. Available online at: http://www.robinalexander.org.uk.

Alexander-Passe, N. (ed.) (2010) *Dyslexia and Creativity: Investigations from Differing Perspectives*. New York: Nova Science Publishers.

Ambrose, P. and Loh, S. C. (2011) 'Effects of the clay modeling program on the reading behaviour of children with dyslexia: a Malaysian case study', *Asia-Pacific Education Researcher*, 20 (3): 456–68.

Bacon, A. and Handley, S. (2010) 'Dyslexia, reasoning and the importance of visual-spatial processes', in N. Alexander-Passe (ed.), *Dyslexia and Creativity: Investigations from Differing Perspectives*. New York: Nova Science Publishers.

Bald, J. (2007) *Using Phonics to Teach Reading and Spelling*. London: Sage.

Barrass, R. (2002) *Scientists Must Write: A Guide to Better Writing for Scientists, Engineers and Students*. London: Routledge.

Bekdemir, M. (2010) 'The pre-service teachers' mathematics anxiety related to depth of negative experiences in mathematics classroom while they were students', *Education Studies in Mathematics*, 75 (3): 311–28.

Bird, R. (2007) *The Dyscalculia Toolkit*. London: Sage.

British Dyslexia Association (BDA) (n.d.) *Dyslexia Research Information*. Available online via 'About Dyslexia' page at: http://www.bdadyslexia.org.uk/.

Brody, L. and Mills, C. (1997) 'Gifted children with learning disabilities: a review of the issues', *Journal of Learning Disabilities*, 30 (3): 282–96.

Butterworth, B. (2003) *Dyscalculia Screener*. London: nferNelson (now GL).

Butterworth, B. (2010) 'Foundational numerical capacities and the origins of dyscalculia', *Trends in Cognitive Science*, 14 (12): 534–41.

Butterworth, B. and Yeo, D. (2004) *Dyscalculia Guidance: Helping Pupils with Specific Learning Difficulties in Math*. London: David Fulton.

Butterworth, B., Varma, S. and Laurillard, D. (2011) 'Dyscalculia: from brain to education', *Science*, 332: 1049–53.

Christ, T. and Wang, X. C. (2012) 'Young children's opportunities to use and learn theme-related vocabulary through buddy "Reading"', *Literacy Research and Instruction*, 51 (4): 273–91.

Clay, M. (1993) *Reading Recovery: A Guidebook for Teachers in Training*. Portsmouth, NH: Heinemann.

Connelly, V., Gee, D. and Walsh, E. (2007) 'A comparison of keyboarded and handwritten compositions and the relationship with transcription speed', *British Journal of Educational Psychology*, 77 (2): 479–92.

Crivelli, V. (2011) *Using ICT to Support Dyslexic Pupils*. Bracknell: BDA New Technologies Committee, British Dyslexia Association. Available online at: http://www.bdadyslexia.org.uk (Information and Activities page, Teachers and Schools menu).

Davis, R. with Braun, E. (1997) *The Gift of Dyslexia*. London: Souvenir Press.

Department for Children, Schools and Families (2009) *Support for Spelling* (2nd edn). Nottingham: DCSF.

Deponio, P. (2004) 'The co-occurrence of specific learning difficulties: implications for identification and assessment', in G. Reid and A. Fawcett (eds), *Dyslexia in Context: Research Policy and Practice*. London: Whurr.

Dockrell, J. and Stuart, M. (2007) *Talking Time*. London: Institute of Education, University of London. Available online at: http://www.ioe.ac.uk/.

Edwards, K. (2008) 'Evaluating the impact of phonics intervention on secondary students' reading improvement', *Education Action Research*, 16 (4): 545–55.

Emmerson, J. and Babtie, P. (2010) *The Dyscalculia Assessment*. London: Continuum.

Ferguson, G. (2006) *Language Planning and Education*. Edinburgh: Edinburgh University Press.

Firman, C. and Francica, C. (2006) 'The position of a dyslexic child exposed to two languages', in S. Tresman and A. Cooke (eds), *The Dyslexia Handbook 2006*. Reading: British Dyslexia Association.

Flint, T. (2010) 'Making meaning together: buddy reading in a first grade classroom', *Early Childhood Education Journal*, 38 (4): 289–97.

Frederickson, N., Frith, U. and Reason, R. (1997) *Phonological Assessment Battery, Manual and Test Materials*. London: GL Assessment.

Gersten, R. and Chard, D. J. (2001) *Number Sense: Rethinking Arithmetic Instruction for Students with Mathematical Disabilities*. Learning Disability on Line. Available online at: http://www.ldonline.org/.

Gillard, J. (2010) 'Developing a National Curriculum that fosters children's creativity', *Learning Matters*, 15 (1): 3–4. Available online at http://www.ceomelb.catholic.edu.au/.

Glynn, T. (2012) Personal communication by email, 21 April.

Glynn, T., Wearmouth, J. and Berryman, M. (2006) *Supporting Students with Literacy Difficulties: A Responsive Approach*. Maidenhead: Open University Press.

Hannell, G. (2005) *Dyscalculia: Action Plans for Successful Learning in Mathematics*. London: David Fulton.

Henley, D. (2012) *Cultural Education in England*. London: Department for Culture, Media and Sport/Department for Education.

House of Commons Children, Schools and Families Committee (2009) *National Curriculum* (Vol. 1, Fourth Report of Session 2008–09). London: TSO.

Jackson, A. (2010) *Being gifted does not guarantee a favourable outcome if you also struggle with dyslexia*. Poster presentation at the British Dyslexia Association, 8th International Conference, Harrogate, June.

Joshi, R. M. and Carreker, S. (2009) 'Spelling: development, assessment and instruction', in G. Reid (ed.), *The Routledge Companion to Dyslexia*. Abingdon: Routledge.

Kelly, K. and Phillips, S. (2011) *Teaching Literacy to Learners with Dyslexia*. London: Sage.

Kirby, A., Sugden, D. and Edwards, L. (2010) 'Developmental co-ordination disorder (DCD): more than just a movement difficulty', *Journal of Research in Special Educational Needs (JORSEN)*, 10 (3): 206–15.

Kiziewicz, M. and Biggs, I. (eds) (2007) *CASCADE: Creativity Across Science, Arts, Dyslexia, Education*. Available online at http://www.bath.ac.uk/.

Landerl, K., Fussenegger, B., Moll, K. and Willburger, E. (2009) 'Dyslexia and dyscalculia: two learning disorders with different cognitive profiles', *Journal of Experimental Child Psychology*, 103 (3): 309–24.

Landon, J. (2001) 'Inclusion and dyslexia – the exclusion of bilingual learners?', in L. Peer and G. Reid (eds), *Dyslexia – Successful Inclusion in the Secondary School*. London: David Fulton.

Lloyd, S. M. (2001) *The Phonics Handbook: A Handbook for Teaching Reading, Writing and Spelling (Jolly Phonics)*. Chigwell: Jolly Learning.

Loew, S. and Watson, K. (2012) 'A prospective genetic marker of the visual-perception disorder Meares-Irlen Syndrome', *Perceptual and Motor Skills*, 114 (3): 870–82.

MacKay, N. (2010) *Taking the Hell Out of Homework*. Wakefield: SEN Marketing.

McKay, N. (2012) *Removing Dyslexia as a Barrier to Achievement* (3rd edn). Wakefield: SEN Marketing. Available online at http://www.senbooks.co.uk.

MacKay, N. and Tresman, S. (2005) *Achieving Dyslexia Friendly Schools Resource Pack*. London: British Dyslexia Association. Available online at: http://www.bdadyslexia.org.uk/ (training and accreditation section).

McKeown, S. (2000) *Dyslexia and ICT: Building on Success*. Coventry: British Educational and Communications Technology Agency (BECTA).

McKissock, C. (2009) *Great Ways to Learn Anatomy and Physiology*. Basingstoke: Palgrave Macmillan.

Meehan, M. M. (2008) *Transitions in Education*. Unpublished paper, Swansea University.

Multiplex Voice Computing Inc. (2012) *MathsTalk™*. Arlington, VT: Multiplex Voice Computing Inc. Available online at: http://www.mathstalk.com/.

National Advisory Committee on Creative and Cultural Education (NACCCE) (1999) *All Our Futures: Creativity, Culture and Education* (The Robinson Report). Available online at: http://www.cypni.org.uk/.

Naylor, S. and Keogh, B. (2010) *Concept Cartoons in Science Education* (rev. edn). Sandbach: Millgate House Education.

Novak, J. (1990) 'Concept mapping: a useful tool for science education', *Journal of Research in Science Teaching*, 27 (10): 937–49.

Nuance Communications Inc. (2012) *Dragon Naturally Speaking*. Marlow: Nuance Communications UK Ltd. Available online at: http://www.nuance.co.uk/.

Office for Standards in Education (Ofsted) (2010) *Reading by Six: How the Best Schools Do It*. Manchester: Ofsted. Available online at: http://www.ofsted.gov.uk.

Office for Standards in Education (Ofsted) (2011) *Removing Barriers to Literacy*. Manchester: Ofsted. Available online at: http://www.ofsted.gov.uk/.

Overington, A. (2012) *A Brief Summary of Government Policy in Relation to EAL Learners*. Available online at: http://www.naldic.org.uk/ (accessed August 2012).

Oxford University Press (n.d.) *Welcome to Numicon*. Kettering: Oxford University Press. Available online at: http://www.numicon.com/.

Pavey, B. (2007) *The Dyslexia-Friendly Primary School*. London: Paul Chapman.

Pavey, B., Meehan, M. and Waugh, A. (2010) *Dyslexia-Friendly Further and Higher Education*. London: Sage.

Peer, L. and Reid, G. (2001) *Dyslexia–Successful Inclusion in the Secondary School*. London: David Fulton.

Pumfrey, P. (1985) *Reading: Tests and Assessment Techniques* (2nd edn). Sevenoaks: Hodder & Stoughton.

Reed, D., Wexler, J. and Vaughn, S. (2012) *RTI for Reading at the Secondary Level*. New York: Guilford Press.

Reid, G. (2009) *Dyslexia, A Practitioner's Handbook*, Chichester: Wiley-Blackwell.

Riddick, B. (2010) *Living With Dyslexia* (2nd edn). Abingdon: Routledge.

Rooms, M. (2000) 'Information and communication technology and dyslexia', in J. Townend and M. Turner (eds), *Dyslexia in Practice: A Guide for Teachers*. New York: Kluwer Academic/ Plenum.

Rose, Sir J. (2006) *Independent Review of the Teaching of Early Reading*. Nottingham: Department for Education and Skills.

Rose, Sir J. (2009) *Identifying and Teaching Children and Young People with Dyslexia and Literacy Difficulties*. Nottingham: DCSF Publications.

Rubinstein, O. and Tannock, R. (2010) 'Mathematics anxiety in children with developmental dyscalculia', *Behavioral and Brain Functions*, 6: 46.

Schneider, E.(2009) 'Dyslexia and foreign language learning', in G. Reid (ed.), *The Routledge Companion to Dyslexia*. Abingdon, Routledge.

Serrano-Lopez, M. and Poehner, M. (2008) 'Materializing linguistic concepts through 3-D clay modeling: a tool-and-result approach to mediating L2 Spanish development', in J. P. Landoff and M. E. Poehner (eds), *Sociocultural Theory and the Teaching of Second Languages*. London: Equinox.

Smedt, B. and Boets, B. (2010) 'Phonological processing and arithmetic fact retrieval: evidence from developmental dyslexia', *Neuropsychologia*, 48 (14): 3973–81.

Smit, M., (n.d.) *Talk for Learning*. PowerPoint presentation. Available online at: http://www.naptec.org.uk.

Spooner, W. (2006) *The SEN Handbook for Trainee Teachers, NQTs and Teaching Assistants*. London: David Fulton.

Tan, S. (2010) 'Singapore's educational reforms: the case for un-standardizing curriculum and reducing testing', *Journal of Scholarship and Practice*, 6 (4): 50–8.

Tanner, E., Brown, A., Day, N., Kotecha, M., Low, N., Morell, G., Turczuk, O., Brown, V., Collingwood, A., Chowdry, H., Greaves, E., Harrison, C., Johnson, G. and Purdon, S. (2011) *Evaluation of Every Child a Reader* (ECaR). London: Department for Education. Available online at: https://www.education.gov.uk/publications/.

Thompson, M. (2009) Editorial note, *Dyslexia*, 15: 147–54.

Tienken, C. and Zhao, Y. (2010) 'Common Core National Curriculum Standards: more questions . . . and answers' (editorial), *Journal of Scholarship and Practice*, 6 (4): 3–13.

Trott, C. and Beacham, N. (2006) 'Project report: wider use of DyscalculiUM: an electronic screening tool for dyscalculia in HE', *Maths Stats & OR Network Connections*, 6 (2): 1–8.

Ullman, M. (2004) 'Contributions of memory circuits to language: the declarative/procedural model', *Cognition*, 92: 231–70.

Vatterott, C. (2010) '5 hallmarks of good homework', *Education Leadership*, 68 January 10–15.

Wadlington, E., Elliott, C. and Kirylo, J. (2008) 'The dyslexia simulation: impact and implications', *Literacy Research and Instruction*, 47 (4): 264–72.

West, T. (1997) *In the Mind's Eye: Visual Thinkers, Gifted People with Dyslexia and Other Learning Difficulties, Computer Images and the Ironies of Creativity*. Amherst, NY: Prometheus Books.

Wilkins, A. J. and Evans, B. J. W. (2009) 'Visual stress, its treatment with spectral filters, and its relationship to visually induced motion sickness', *Applied Ergonomics*, 41 (4): 509–15.

Williams, P. (2008) *Independent Review of Mathematics Teaching in Early Years Settings and Primary Schools*. London: Department of Children, Schools and Families.

Wolff, U. (2010) 'Artistic talents and dyslexia: a genuine connection?', in N. Alexander-Passe (ed.), *Dyslexia and Creativity: Investigations from Differing Perspectives*. New York: Nova Science.

Wyse, D. and Jones, R. (2008) *Teaching English, Language and Literacy* (2nd edn). Abingdon: Routledge.

Zamach, M. (1993) *The Little Red Hen: An Old Story*. New York: Farrar, Strauss & Giroux (Sunburst Paperbacks).

Ziegler, J. and Goswami, U. (2005) 'Reading acquisition, developmental dyslexia, and skilled reading across languages: a psycholinguistic grain size theory', *Psychological Bulletin*, 131 (1): 3–29.

Index